SUDOKU

CROSSWORDS   WOS

LOGIC PUZZLES   &

minD
STRETCHERS

VOLUME 2

EDITED BY ALLEN D. BRAGDON

Reader's
digest

New York / Montreal

Copyright © 2017 by Trusted Media Brands, Inc.

ISBN 978-1-62145-374-1

Address any comments about *Mind Stretchers Volume 2* to:

Reader's Digest Adult Trade Books
44 South Broadway, 7th Floor
White Plains, NY 10601

Visit us on the Web:
rd.com (in the United States)
readersdigest.ca (in Canada)

Printed in China

10 9 8 7 6 5

Contents

Dear Puzzler,

Genealogy—the study of families and tracing of their lineages—is something that puzzlers are good at. It's detective work, like putting a jigsaw together and following leads and clues, and each new piece of information gleaned is a triumph.

The Internet has vastly increased the resources available and there has been an explosion of interest in the subject, but still some good old-fashioned legwork is sometimes required.

Like that undertaken by the young man searching for the grave of his famous, but long lost, great uncle. He narrowed the search down by reading the local newspaper reports in search of an obituary and even found a plan of the most likely cemetery at the local library, and set off on his mission.

On arrival at the cemetery, imagine his consternation and absolute frustration to find that the whole layout had been reorganized to maximize the ground space, and all the older untended memorials had been moved to create a neat grid pattern to one side. Row after row of memorials.

After much fruitless searching, peering to read the fading inscriptions in vain, with the light fading, one of the groundskeepers noticed him, came over and asked if he could be of any assistance.

Our man looked at him gratefully and said, "Yes, I'm trying to find the memorial to a relation of mine. It makes some mention of the fact that he invented the cryptic crossword puzzle."

"Oh that one!" replied the groundskeeper immediately. "That's easy to find," he said, pointing. "It's ten down and sixteen across!"

Allen D. Bragdon
Mind Stretchers Puzzle Editor

■ Meet the Authors

Allen D. Bragdon

Allen describes himself as "the whimsical old dog with puzzle experience and a curious mind." He is a member of the Society for Neuroscience, founding editor of *Games* magazine and editor of the Playspace daily puzzle column, formerly syndicated internationally by *The New York Times*. The author of dozens of books of professional and academic examinations and how-to instructions in practical skills, Allen is also the director of the Brainwaves Center.

PeterFrank

PeterFrank was founded in 2000. It is a partnership between High Performance bvba, owned by Peter De Schepper, and Frank Coussement bvba, owned by Frank Coussement. Together they form a dynamic, full-service content provider specialized in media content.They have more than 20 years of experience in publishing management, art/design and software development for newspapers, consumer magazines, special interest publications and new media.

John M. Samson

John M. Samson is currently editor of Simon & Schuster's *Mega Crossword Series*. His crosswords have appeared on cereal boxes, rock album covers, quilts, jigsaw puzzles, posters, advertisements, newspapers, magazines ... and sides of buildings. John also enjoys painting and writing for the stage and screen.

Sam Bellotto Jr.

Sam Bellotto Jr. has been making puzzles professionally since 1979, when he broke into the business by placing his first sale with *The New York Times Magazine*, under then crossword puzzle editor Eugene T. Maleska. Sam has been a regular contributor to Simon & Schuster, *The New York Times*, Random House, and magazines such as *Back Stage*, *Central New York*, *Public Citizen* and *Music Alive!* Bellotto's Rochester, NY-based company, Crossdown, develops word-puzzle computer games and crossword construction software.

When Sam is not puzzling he's out hiking with Petra, his black Labrador dog.

BrainSnack®

The internationally registered trademark BrainSnack® stands for challenging, language-independent, logic puzzles and mind games for kids, young adults and adults. The brand stands for high-quality puzzles. Whether they are made by hand, such as visual puzzles, or generated by a computer, such as sudoku, all puzzles are tested by the target group they are made for before they are made available. In order to guarantee that computer-generated puzzles can actually be solved by humans, BrainSnack® makes programs that only use human logic algorithms.

◼ Meet the Puzzles

Mind Stretchers is filled with a delightful mix of classic and new puzzle types. To help you get started, here are instructions for each, with tips and examples included.

WORD GAMES

Crossword Puzzles

Clues. Clues. Clues.

Clues are the deciding factor that determines crossword-solving difficulty. Many solvers mistakenly think strange and unusual words are what make a puzzle challenging. In reality, crossword constructors generally try to avoid grid esoterica, opting for familiar words and expressions.

For example, here are some actual clues you'll be encountering and their respective difficulty levels:

LEVEL 1   Eggplant color

LEVEL 2   Plane for quick takeoffs

LEVEL 3   Salinger dedicatee

LEVEL 4   Run roughly, as an engine

LEVEL 5   Pedicab kin

Clues to amuse. Clues to educate. Clues to challenge your mind.

All the clues are there—what's needed now is your answers.

Happy solving!

Word Searches

by PeterFrank

Both kids and grown-ups love 'em, making word searches one of the most popular types of puzzle. In a word search, the challenge is to find hidden words within a grid of letters. In the typical puzzle, words can be found in vertical columns, horizontal rows or along diagonals, with the letters of the words running either forward or backward. You'll be given a list of words to find. But it does not stop there. There is a hidden message—related to the theme of the word search—in the letters left behind after all of the clues have been found. String together those extra letters, and the message will reveal itself.

Hints: *One of the most reliable and efficient searching methods is to scan each row from top to bottom for the first letter of the word. So if you are looking for "violin," you would look for the letter "v." When you find one, look at all the letters that surround it for the second letter of the word (in this case, "i"). Each time you find a correct two-letter combination (in this case, "vi"), you can then scan either for the correct three-letter combination ("vio") or the whole word.*

Word Sudoku

by PeterFrank

Sudoku puzzles have become hugely popular, and our word sudoku puzzles bring a much-loved challenge to word puzzlers.

The basic sudoku puzzle is a 9 x 9 square grid, split into 9 square regions, each containing 9 cells. You need to complete the grid so that each row, each column and each 3 x 3 frame contains the nine letters from the black box above the grid.

There is always a hidden nine-letter word in the diagonal from top left to bottom right.

EXAMPLE   **SOLUTION**

NUMBER GAMES

Sudoku

by PeterFrank

The original sudoku number format is amazingly popular the world over due to its simplicity and challenge.

The basic sudoku puzzle is a 9 x 9 square grid, split into 9 square regions, each containing 9 cells. Complete the grid so that each row, each column and each 3 x 3 frame contains every number from 1 to 9.

EXAMPLE   **SOLUTION**

As well as classic sudoku puzzles, you'll also find sudoku X puzzles, where the main diagonals must also include every number from 1 to 9, and sudoku twins with two overlapping grids.

Kakuro

by PeterFrank

These puzzles are like crosswords with numbers. There are clues across and down, but the clues are numbers. The solution is a sum that adds up to the clue number.

Each number in a black area is the sum of the numbers that you have to enter in the empty boxes beside or below. The empty boxes that make up the sum are called a run. The sum of the across run is written above the diagonal in the black area, while the sum of the down run is written below the diagonal.

Runs can contain only the numbers 1 through 9, and each number in a run can only be used once. The gray boxes contain only odd numbers and the white contain only even numbers.

EXAMPLE   **SOLUTION**

LOGIC PUZZLES

Binairo

by PeterFrank

Binairo puzzles look similar to sudoku puzzles. They are just as simple and challenging but that is where the similarity ends.

There are two versions: odd and even. The even puzzles feature a 12 x 12 grid. You need to complete the grid with zeros and ones, until there are 6 zeros and 6 ones in every row and every column. No more than two of the same number can be next to or under each other. Rows or columns with exactly the same combination are not allowed.

<table>
<tr><td>**EXAMPLE**</td><td>**SOLUTION**</td></tr>
</table>

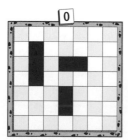

The odd puzzles feature an 11 x 11 grid. You need to complete the grid with zeros and ones until there are 5 zeros and 6 ones in every row and column.

Keep Going

In this puzzle, start on a blank square of your choice and connect as many blank squares as possible with one single continuous line.

You can only connect squares along vertical and horizontal lines, not along diagonals. You must continue the connecting line up until the next obstacle—i.e., the rim of the box, a black square or a square that has already been used.

You can change direction at any obstacle you meet. Each square can be used only once. The number of blank squares left unused is marked in the upper square. There is more than one solution, but we include only one solution in our answer key.

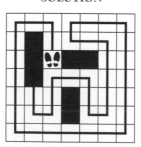

EXAMPLE   **SOLUTION**

Number Cluster

by PeterFrank

Number Cluster puzzles are language-free, logical numerical problems. They consist of cubes on a 6 x 6 grid. Numbers have been placed in some of the cubes, while the rest are empty. Your challenge is to complete the grid by creating runs of the same number and length as the number supplied. So where a cube with the number 5 has been included on the grid, you need to create a run of five number 5s, including the cube already shown. The run can be horizontal, vertical, or both horizontal and vertical.

EXAMPLE   **SOLUTION**

Word Pyramid

Each word in the pyramid has the letters of the word above it, plus a new letter.

Start with the answer to clue No.1 and work your way to the base of the pyramid to complete the word pyramid.

Sport Maze

This puzzle is presented on a 6 x 6 grid. Your starting point is indicated by a red cell with a ball and a number. Your objective is to draw the shortest route from the ball to the goal, the only square without a number. You can only move along vertical and horizontal lines, not along diagonals. The figure on each square indicates the number of squares the ball must be moved in the same direction. You can change direction at each stop.

EXAMPLE   SOLUTION

Cage the Animals

This puzzle presents you with a zoo divided into a 16 x 16 grid. The different animals on the grid need to be separated. Draw lines that will completely divide up the grid into smaller squares, with exactly one animal per square. The squares should not overlap.

EXAMPLE   SOLUTION

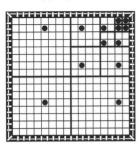

Throughout *Mind Stretchers* you will find unique mazes, visual conundrums and other colorful challenges. Each comes with a new name and unique instructions. Our best advice? Patience and perseverance. Your eyes will need time to unravel the visual secrets.

BrainSnack® Puzzles

To solve a BrainSnack® puzzle, you must think logically. You'll need to use one or several strategies to detect direction, differences and/or similarities, associations, calculations, order, spatial insight, colors, quantities and distances. A BrainSnack® ensures that all the brain's capacities are fully engaged. These are brain sports at their best!

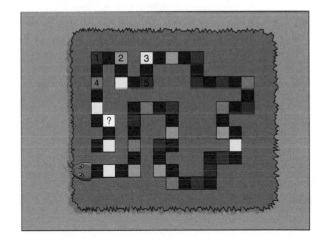

Find the Right Word

Can you find a word within this grid? Arrows are scattered on the grid. Each arrow points toward a letter that is part of the solution word, but the letters cannot be next to each other vertically, horizontally or diagonally.

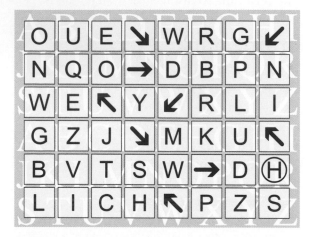

You'll also find more than 100 short brain-teasers scattered throughout these pages. These puzzles, found at the bottom of the page, will give you a little light relief from the more intense puzzles while still challenging you.

• ONE LETTER LESS OR MORE

T R I A N G L E ⊕L ☐ R ☐ ☐ ☐ ☐

• LETTERBLOCKS

B A A E O R C
E T Z T P A R

• BLOCK ANAGRAM

SOLAR TIE *(played by one person)*

☐ ☐ ☐ ☐ ☐ ☐ **I** ☐ ☐

• DOODLE PUZZLE

P ≠ ⚽

But wait—there's more!

There are additional brainteasers at the top of odd numbered pages, organized into two categories:

• **QUICK!:** These tests challenge your ability to instantly calculate numbers or recall well-known facts.

• **DO YOU KNOW...:** These more demanding questions probe the depth of your knowledge of facts and trivia.

■ Master Class: To the Point

A Penknife, Bread and Octopus—the Puzzler's Friends

We take it all for granted really. Here we are with our volume of Mind Stretchers in hand, mechanical pencil at the ready—the eraser at the end as we chew over the crossword clues, then fill in an answer—only to write in another that doesn't fit with that one. Rethink—then erase it, write in another.

All of the mechanics are there. The paper surface, intentionally slightly rough to accept the marks we can make and remove with such ease.

How did we get to this point?

A little archaeology reveals some answers.

"Literature," from the Latin *literatura*, corresponds in meaning to the Anglo-Saxon "writing."

Litteratura, generalization of *littera*, means "body or system of letters." But what is *littera*, a single letter? It means originally "smearing"—from *litus*, "smeared."

"Writing," on the other hand means, properly, *"scratching"* or *"scoring"*—from the Anglo-Saxon *writan*, "to score"—a word comparable in certain respects to the Swedish *rita*, "to draw"; Dutch *riijten*, "to split"; the Old High German *rizan*, (Modern German *reissen)*, "to tear."

Book, again, is the Anglo-Saxon *boc*, "a beech-tree," just as the German *buch*, "a book," is but a reduced form of *buche*, "beech-tree," The Latin for book is *liber*, the bark or rind of a tree, and *library* means properly "a body or system of rinds." In Greek, too, book is *biblos*, a word which denotes the inner bark of the papyrus. "Bible" is, therefore, properly "bark," and *bibliotheke* (the Greek for library or bookcase) "system of barks."

But what has literature to do with smearing or writing with scratching? Or, what has book to do with beech? Or liber with bark, or library with a collection of barks?

Like every other art, literature or writing began in a very humble way. To make signs or characters to represent things they wanted to call to mind, man began by scratching figures of them on stone or clay, or by *scratching* or *smearing* them on leather or other such material.

Our word "book" comes from a time when runes or written characters were cut into slabs of beechwood.

The Greek *grapheion,* the Latin *stylus* (from where we get our word "style"), both meaning "a pen," was a hard instrument of metal or ivory with which characters were scratched into a tablet. The tablet of wood was covered with a thin layer of wax and enclosed by a raised rim. The writing was scored into the layer of wax by means of the sharp end of the style, and, by using the broad upper end of the style, the characters could be erased. Such tablets were used in schools and also for ordinary letters and dispatches.

Joined together by wires or rings, serving as hinges, two or more tablets formed a *codex*—a book made up of a number of sheets.

By means of their clay tablets, the Babylonians, too, at a much earlier date, carried on lively correspondence with all parts of the East. In Egypt there have been found a great number of potsherds or *ostraka* bearing on them inscriptions either scratched with a sharp point or written in ink with a reed. Most of these are receipts for taxes, and were probably carried by donkeys when the collectors went on their rounds gathering taxes. Wax tablets continued to be written upon until as late as the 15th century A.D. Some examples still survive in Florence.

Another method was, not to scratch the characters on wood or bark or similar material, but to *smear* them on the dressed skin or leather of calf, sheep or goat. It is called *parchment*.

Many early parchment manuscripts were recycled by scrubbing and scouring to be made ready for rewriting, and often the earlier writing can still be read. These recycled parchments are known as *palimpsests*.

Our word "paper" comes from the Egyptian *papyrus*. The early Egyptians cut very thin slices of the stem of the papyrus plant vertically and in order to use them as material on which characters were drawn. Rolls of charactered (or written) papyrus constituted, in early times, a book.

Many such papyri have been found in Egypt, as well as places outside of Egypt where they had been imported, such as at Herculaneum and Pompeii. Papyrus was a very useful material. Ancient Egyptians used this plant not only as a writing material, but for making boats, mattresses, mats, rope, sandals and baskets.

We still make use of the word "volume" (i.e. *roll,* our word "voluminous" still meaning *roll-ful),* though today our "volumes" are oblong in shape and no longer roll but lie flat. The "rolls of Court" and "rolls of Parliament" for example are parchments (in *rolls*) which record the various acts and proceedings of the body in question.

The earliest inscriptions still in existence are characters engraved on stone, such as those found in Egypt. Papyrus was, however, also in use in Egypt as a writing material from a very early date. The *Prisse Papyrus,* dating from the twelfth dynasty Egyptian Middle Kingdom, is one of the earliest surviving papyrus documents.

Some of the earliest writings in existence are Mesopotamian. The Sumerians are often described as having the earliest known written language. Examples of its earliest, logographic form (where a single symbol was used to represent a whole word), date back to as far as 3500 B.C.

A more advanced stage of writing in Sumer is shown in later cuneiform (i.e. wedge-shaped) inscriptions. These were scored into tablets of clay while soft, which, after being marked, were sun-dried or kiln-baked. Mesopotamian correspondence was an interchange of such tablets.

The oldest Greek records are inscriptions in stone or metal; but Greek papyri dating from the 2nd century B.C. have also been unearthed.

Under the empire nine different kinds of papyri were prepared and used in Rome. A process of bleaching, invented after the time of Augustus, turned out a papyrus superior to the best Egyptian kind. The two best were called the *Charta Augusta* (used only for letters) and the *Charta Livia*. A papyrus library of around 2,000 rolls, ranged in presses along the sides of the room, was uncovered at Herculaneum.

Papyrus records survive today from 5th century A.D. imperial rescripts; of 5th-to-10th-century Ravenna deeds; of 7th-century Merovingian charters; and of 11th-century Papal Chancery documents.

The use of parchment as a writing material derives from the city of Pergamon, in Asia Minor, and is believed to date from about 190 B.C. In the case of parchment, the leather was prepared so that both sides were available for writing. The older form of leather was usable on only one side.

Parchment or vellum (i.e. calfskin) continued to be the usual material for books from the 4th to the 16th century. Paper (deriving its name from *papyrus*), at first made of vegetable fiber, was manufactured by Arabs about 800 A.D., was used in France for deeds in the 13th century, and was made in England by John Tate in the 15th century.

The earliest device for writing was probably the brush, still used by the Chinese and Japanese. (It is interesting that a "pencil" formerly was a small, finely-pointed brush used for delicate work in watercolor painting.)

Characters were inscribed on papyrus or parchment by means of a reed (*calamus, fistula, canna*) cut to a point and dipped in ink. The ink was made of soot and gum, or of the juice of a cuttlefish. Cuttlefish ink used to be an important dye, called *sepia*. (These days,

artificial dyes have replaced natural sepia.) Later, ink was made of iron and gallnut. The latter, not erasable, was the only kind of ink used for parchment.

The quill or pen (from *penna,* "a feather") is first referred to as an instrument of writing by Isidore of Seville in the 7th century. By the 13th century, the pen (or quill) had superseded the reed in Europe.

Quills were made from a primary feather of a bird's wing. Swan, goose and turkey provided the best quill pens. The quill was prepared by heating it in sand and then scraping off the soft outer skin. Knives were formerly carried especially for the purpose of sharpening quill pens. In modern times, the name of *penknife* is still applied to a small pocketknife.

The metal pen, or nib, as we commonly call it, first came into use about 1830. Ordinary pens were made of steel and took many forms, from fine pens used in cartography to those used by sign-writers. Then came the fountain pen with its ink reservoir.

Ballpoint pens are widely referred to as "Biros" in many English-speaking countries. For that we thank László József Bíró—the inventor of the modern ballpoint pen, which first saw the light of day in 1931, was patented in 1938 and is now part of the Bic Company.

Looking at different inks, Bíró developed a pen with a new tip made of a rolling ball that was free to turn in a socket. As it rolled, the ball picked up ink from a reservoir cartridge, and the ink rolled onto the writing surface.

It was not until the 16th century that pencils were produced. A deposit of graphite was discovered in England during the first half of the 1500s. It was cut into sticks and used to mark sheep. It was believed that the graphite was lead—and the word *lead* has been used to describe pencils ever since then.

Around 1560, Italian couple Simonio and Lyndiana Bernacotti invented the pencil by placing graphite sticks inside hollowed-out wood. Later, an improved technique evolved where the graphite stick was placed between two wooden halves that were then joined together.

There are many forms of pencil where the graphite is contained in a holder and can be drawn back or thrust forward mechanically.

Many puzzlers these days use a mechanical or propelling pencil with an eraser attached.

Before rubber erasers were invented, tablets of rubber or wax were used to erase lead or charcoal marks from paper. Small pieces of rough stone, such as sandstone or pumice were used to correct errors or remove marks from parchment and papyrus documents written with ink.

Artists used rolled-up balls of bread as an eraser that could remove chalk, charcoal and pencil marks. Some still do, but an English engineer, Edward Nairne, gets the credit for developing the rubber eraser around 1770, having picked up a piece of rubber instead of his bread ball and discovering that it did the trick.

In 1858, Hymen Lipman from Philadelphia came up with the idea of attaching an eraser to the end of a pencil—genius really—the must-have tool for any word puzzler—but it was to be another fifty years before Arthur Wynne invented the first crossword puzzle, published on Sunday December 21, 1913 in the *New York World*.

So don't be stuck with your *Mind Stretchers* puzzles. If you make a mistake and you have chewed the eraser from your pencil, go and find some bread.

If you can't find a pencil or your pen runs out, just pop out and get some cuttlefish or squid, or an octopus will do nicely.

★ Opposite Numbers by Michele Sayer

ACROSS

1 Apple variety
5 "On ___ Boat to China"
10 Leave left unsaid
14 Southern U.S. hwy.
15 Artemis, to the Romans
16 Fashion designer Gernreich
17 Coiffure crisis
19 Bikini component
20 Not in harm's way
21 Pugsley's uncle
23 Small bays
24 Biblical angel wrestler
25 Forgets to play it cool
28 Spouses
31 Reduce
32 Live stream component
33 Journalist Hentoff
34 Costello and Ferrigno
35 Playful hop
36 *Rent* heroine
37 Toby, for one
38 Arranged for a photo
39 Georgia city
40 Olympics entrants
42 "As if that ___ enough ..."
43 Revival shelters
44 Muralist Chagall
45 Milano in *Hall Pass*
47 Mirrors
51 Lays down the lawn
52 1990 De Niro film
54 Sunblock ingredient
55 Message from Amazon
56 Draw in outline
57 Use the beeper
58 In the mean time
59 Pre-splat cry

DOWN

1 Little lies
2 Beehive state
3 *Star Wars* knight
4 Acquires genetically
5 Nike rival
6 Fathers
7 Diane in *Wild at Heart*
8 *Snakes ___ Plane* (2006)
9 Wandering one
10 It's said in church
11 2005 Lyfe Jennings song
12 Twiddling one's thumbs
13 Piece of cake
18 Wonderland lass
22 Opposite of endo
24 Beyond blasé
25 Majorcan seaport
26 Roughly
27 Scolding for Fido
28 They're calling Danny Boy
29 Novarro of silents
30 Stretch in the service
32 Ming artifacts
35 Small country houses
36 Mastroianni in *8½*
38 Bic products
39 Haggard who sang "Mama Tried"
41 One paying a flat fee
42 Breakfast order
44 *M*A*S*H* worker
45 Quick like a bunny!
46 *Kinky Boots* cabaret singer
47 Gray-sorrel
48 Mother of Hyacinth
49 Pipe smoker's tool
50 ID-theft targets
53 German grandmother

★ BrainSnack®—Keep Turning

Which wheel (1–5) doesn't belong to the set?

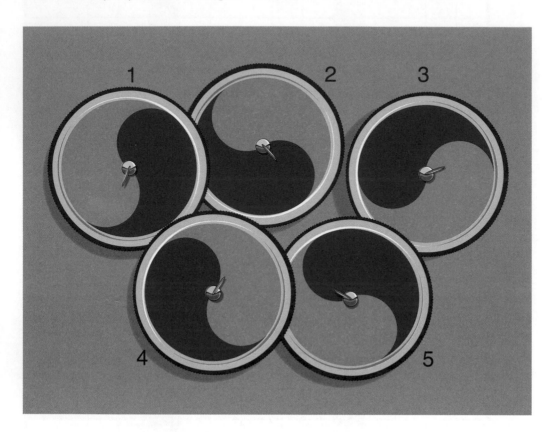

CLOCKWISE

The answers to the clues from 1 to 12 are all seven-letter words that end with the letter E. When you have solved the puzzle correctly, working clockwise from 1, the twelve letters in the outer circle will spell a word meaning "miserly."

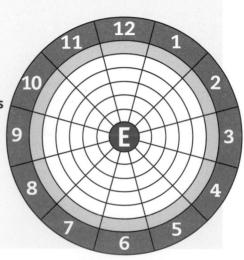

1 Voluntary self-punishment
2 To release from blame, pardon
3 Joplin's jazz style
4 Unequally-sided triangle
5 Revere
6 Gruesome "danse"
7 Consisting of eight parts
8 Candidate
9 Vexing, tedious
10 Former
11 Hawaiian guitar
12 Vatican chapel

★ Art Trends

All the words are hidden vertically, horizontally or diagonally—in both directions. The letters that remain unused form a sentence from left to right.

```
L A M R O F N I D A D A I S M
J U G E N D S T I L C A R A V
A G G E U Q S E N A M O R I S
B T I W E C N A S S I A N E R
E O M S I L A E R R E S M M C
T Y D B A U H A U S M L S S L
A I G Y S T I B C A S F I I A
O N L O A L O S O S I A B V S
W E I R T R S T C S N R U I S
G O T M F H T R O E O T C T I
R A R S I T I A C M I N H C C
A R A I E S E C O B S O I U I
F T P T M T M T R L S U A R S
F D O E P L I A A A E V N T M
I E P I I B A R R G R E O S Q
T C U P R E P T A E P A I N N
I O T E E R C A R A X U V O A
G G M S I R A L U C E S I C O
```

CUBISM
DADAISM
EMPIRE
EXPRESSIONISM
GOTHIC
GRAFFITI
INFORMAL
JUGENDSTIL
PIETISM
POP ART
REALISM
RENAISSANCE
ROCOCO
ROMANESQUE
SECULARISM

ABSTRACT ART | ART NOUVEAU | BODY ART
ANIMISM | ASSEMBLAGE | CLASSICISM
ART DECO | BAUHAUS | CONSTRUCTIVISM

TRIANAGRAM

Three-word groups of anagrams are called triplets or trianagrams.
Complete the group:

TEARING _ _ _ _ _ _ _   _ _ _ _ _ _ _

★ Hot and Cold by Michele Sayer

ACROSS

1 "Amo, amas, I love a ___": O'Keeffe
5 Morph into
11 1970 Jackson 5 hit
14 Spicy stew
15 X-rated
16 ___-di-dah
17 Living dangerously
20 S&L part
21 Madcap trio
22 Org. once represented by Heston
23 Bond villain Blofeld
24 Like eggshells
28 "The Sweetest Taboo" singer
30 Tupperware top
31 Deep Throat, notably
33 Brief set-to
37 "Gotcha," to a beatnik
39 Disney's lion king
40 Hurly-burly
41 Fleshy fruit
42 Word with rush or happy
43 Give one star to
44 Help with the job
46 Plato's school
50 Flora and fauna of a region
53 Ending denoting origin
54 Conclusions
57 Like macramé
61 1968 Rock Hudson film
63 Breadbasket
64 Homecoming figures
65 Leave the dock
66 Double curve in the road
67 Conduct
68 Fairway obstacle

DOWN

1 Takes a bough?
2 ___ breve (2/2 time)
3 Pole or Czech
4 Saw
5 Tiger of India
6 10 million equal a joule
7 "How now brown ___?"
8 Sheriff Taylor kept a cell for him
9 Goalie glove
10 Resounded
11 Associate (with)
12 Undresses
13 Box for a pirate
18 Letters at Calvary
19 Timberland
24 Go crazy, slangily
25 Midway amusement
26 Top 5 song by Sarah McLachlan
27 *Silas Marner* author
28 Native-born Israeli
29 Pseudonymous letters
32 Outback ratite
34 Catholic leader
35 Composer de la Halle
36 Cousin of an Obie
38 For free
39 Haggard novel
45 Big name in paperbacks
47 Basketball Hall-of-Famer Hawkins
48 Whole ball of wax
49 View with loathing
50 Grayish-brown
51 Aural anvil
52 *Waiting for Lefty* playwright
55 Society-page fodder
56 Leave thunderstruck
57 King on Skull Island
58 It can give you a lift
59 Albany-to-Buffalo canal
60 Racer Earnhardt
62 "___ little teapot ..."

★★ Keep Going

Start on a blank square of your choice and connect as many blank squares as possible with one single continuous line. You can only connect squares along vertical and horizontal lines. You must continue the connecting line up until the next obstacle, i.e., the rim of the box, a black square or a square that has already been used. You can change direction at any obstacle you meet. Each square can be used only once. The number of blank squares that will be left unused is marked in the upper square. There is more than one solution. We show only one solution.

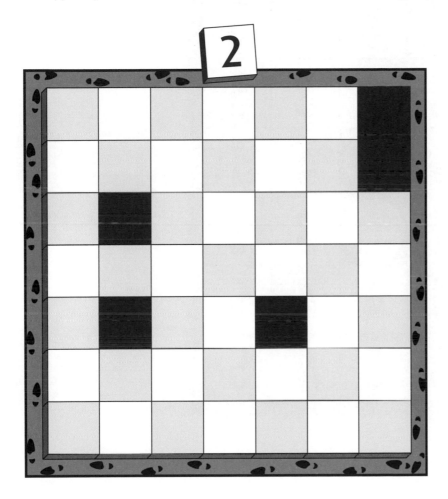

FRIENDS?

What do the following words have in common?

RIG HUM RAP LIMP SOL

★★★ Sport Maze

Draw the shortest way from the ball to the goal. You can only move along vertical and horizontal lines, not along diagonal lines. The figure on each square indicates the number of squares the ball must be moved in the same direction. You can change direction at each stop.

4	4	4	4	2	5
2	2	4	4	3	5
4	3	1	2	4	1
4	4	1	●	3	5
4	1	4	4	4	5
3	2	3	5	4	5

ONE LETTER LESS OR MORE

The word on the right side contains the letters of the word on the left side plus or minus the letter in the middle. One letter is already in the right place.

★ For Good Measure by Mary Leonard

ACROSS
1 *Man and Superman* playwright
5 Snooze ___
10 Disposable razor
14 Modeled
15 Opera singer Lanza
16 Cauterize
17 *Guys and Dolls* song
20 Where to find Helena
21 Erases
22 "___ tu" (*A Masked Ball* aria)
23 Puerto ___
24 Spies seek them
28 Emulated Mme. Defarge
31 North Carolina campus
32 Munchausen's repertoire
34 "One day only!" event
35 ___ Supply of rock fame
36 Jeans label
37 Spy novelist Deighton
38 Like the Texas star
40 They sang with the Papas
42 Certain subdivision
43 At a loss
45 Leaves
47 IRS functionaries
48 14, in old Rome
49 Impolite
52 Cartography volumes
56 UK volume measures
58 Toastmaster's spot
59 Not from around here
60 Granny's other daughter
61 Groups of epochs
62 Raise the flag
63 Hot tubs

DOWN
1 Emulated Missy Franklin
2 Bindlestiff
3 "Make ___ for it!"
4 Omelet type
5 First-class hotel offering
6 "Ooh ___!"
7 Sky altar
8 Edam exterior
9 Contemporary people
10 Parts
11 Nondrinker
12 Pimlico event
13 Torah chests
18 One with big ears
19 Others, in the Forum
24 Barkers
25 *Adam Bede* novelist
26 Horn of plenty
27 Vegetable dish
28 Homophone of need
29 Word on political pins
30 Fender flaws
33 "Radio Song" group
39 Catherine I, for one
40 Promised one
41 Celestial navigation tool
42 *Kojak* star
44 Brace
46 Caplet
49 Hang fire
50 Vizquel of baseball
51 Sundog
52 Becomes ripe
53 First course option
54 Birthplace of Ceres
55 Former jet-set jets
57 Weeks in a Julian calendar

★ BrainSnack®—Buzzzzz

Bees 1 and 2 are a couple. Which two other bees (3–7) are also a couple?

LETTER LINE

Put a letter in each of the squares below to make a word that means "prognosticator." The number clues refer to other words that can be made from the whole.

2 8 1 4 9 10 EDIBLE MARINE MOLLUSC;
7 1 1 9 10 4 INSIST UPON;
10 7 6 5 IMPETUOUS, OVERHASTY; 9 7 10 4 5 8 ROBUST;
UNREFINED; 4 2 10 1 3 TRUNK

1	2	3	4	5	6	7	8	9	10

★ Word Sudoku

Complete the grid so that each row, each column and each 3 x 3 frame contains the nine letters from the black box below. The hidden nine-letter word is in the diagonal from top left to bottom right.

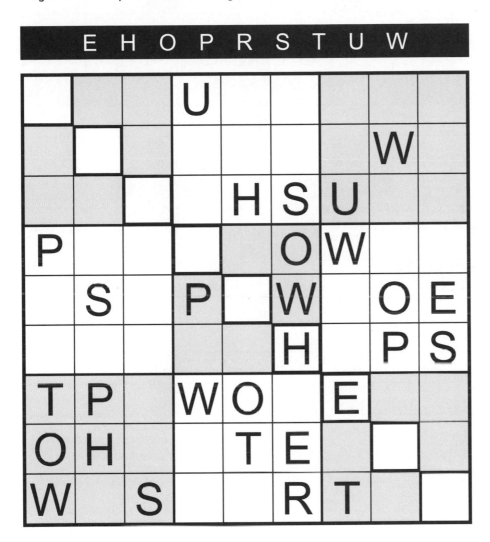

E H O P R S T U W

UNCANNY TURN

Rearrange the letters of the phrase below to form a cognate anagram, one which is related or connected in meaning to the original phrase. The answer can be one or more words.

TRIMS CASH

★ Patriotic Songs by Don Law

ACROSS

1 Beaver Cleaver's dad
5 30-day trial versions, e.g.
10 Pipe part
14 His, in Paris
15 Public notice
16 Nasty guy
17 Patriotic London song
20 Ben in *Zoolander*
21 Rich
22 Suffix with different
23 Withheld
24 "Old Hickory" president
28 Spots
32 Amor's wings
33 Butter ___ ice cream
35 Wetlands wader
36 Eskimo food cutter
37 Nala's foot
38 When Sergius III assumed the papacy
39 Tammany Hall caricaturist
41 Spy in Canaan
43 Loads
44 Hang-gliding current
46 Mailing out
48 Ending for velvet
49 Dot partner
50 Work on a Pixar movie
54 Token amount
58 Patriotic New York song
60 Knavish
61 Sentimentalize
62 *Volsunga Saga* king
63 "Mermaid" singer
64 Where to find fulmars
65 Low-fat

DOWN

1 Wits
2 "Thanks ___!"
3 Monokini designer Gernreich
4 Antipathy
5 Slowly come to light
6 Feeder of the Fulda
7 School near Harvard
8 Eight in Madrid
9 His feast day is December 26
10 Rock that won't roll
11 Double-curve molding
12 *Beau Geste* novelist
13 Shrove Tuesday follower
18 Sigh of pity
19 Cry uncle
24 Day trip
25 God, to many
26 ___ célèbre
27 Site of Edmund Hillary's base camp
28 Rachel in *Batman Begins*
29 Mojave plants
30 *The Lion King* meerkat
31 Throw mud
34 Hockley in *Titanic*
40 Appear cold
41 Soldier's flask
42 Flatters
43 Officer of the fleet
45 Happy or square follower
47 Lymph bump
50 Eternities
51 PBS science series
52 "What ___ for Love"
53 Farmer's wife in *Babe*
54 Fictional spy Helm
55 Mention in a footnote
56 Campus near Beverly Hills
57 Primary water pipe
59 Urgent call for help

★ Sudoku

Fill in the grid so that each row, each column and each 3 x 3 frame contains every number from 1 to 9.

							8	
			6					5
4						7		1
	5		7		9			
	3	8	4					
9		6				5		
8					1	2		
5	6	2	9	8	4		3	
	7	3	5	6	2			4

SYMBOL SUMS

Can you work out these number sums using three of these four symbols? **+ − ÷ ×**
(No fractions or minus numbers are involved in the sum as you progress from left to right.)

$$32 \ \square \ 8 \ \square \ 5 \ \square \ 3 = 24$$

★★ Find the Right Word

Knowing that every arrow points to a letter and that no letter can touch another vertically, horizontally or diagonally, find the missing letters that form a keyword in reading direction. A letter cannot be located on an arrow. We show one letter in a circle to help you get started.

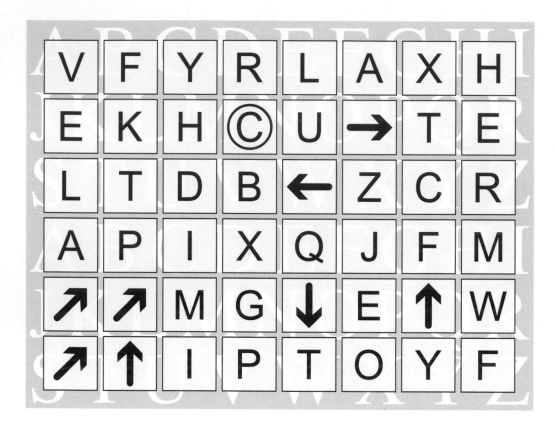

CHANGELINGS

Each of the three lines of letters below spell words that have a school connection, but the letters have been mixed up. Four letters from the first word are now in the third line, four letters from the third word are in the second line and four letters from the second word are in the first line. The remaining letters are in their original places. What are the words?

C S A L E B O N R T
A C S R S S M E O M
H L A S S K O A D S

★ Broadway Musicals I by Linda Lather

ACROSS

1 Manet's "___ at the Folies-Bergère"
5 Merman in *Gypsy*
10 Swaddle
14 Neck area
15 Green dough
16 Locale of some Swiss banks?
17 "Hello" musical
20 Imitated a peacock
21 Jostled
22 ___ and there
23 Over and done with
24 Expected to happen
27 Art lover
31 Oven alarm
32 Boating rates
33 ___ of La Mancha
34 *Tempus edax rerum* writer
35 Sierra ___
36 Openly grieved
37 Ryan in *Top Gun*
38 Humdinger
39 See-through
40 Likely to happen
42 Fortified wine
43 Cross letters
44 Kenton of jazz
45 Puckered fabric
48 Where to find the Ponte Vecchio
52 "Surrender" musical
54 Dutch singer DeLange
55 Inflexible
56 Chisholm Trail town
57 ATM feature
58 Pledges
59 Optimistic

DOWN

1 Echidna's dinner
2 Thailand currency
3 Copycat
4 Answered a debater
5 Chewed the scenery
6 Subway tender
7 Hooligan
8 Will Ferrell film
9 Light into
10 Fireside feeling
11 Way on or off
12 Island group off of New Guinea
13 Be up in the air
18 Follower of each or no
19 Banishes
23 Large flower
24 Bang your boot
25 Variety meat
26 Chihuahua chum
27 Chameleon
28 Arab head of state
29 Get to the point?
30 Port of ___
32 Kuehne of the LPGA
35 Broadway musical book
36 At any time
38 ___ *Macabre*: Saint-Saëns
39 Split the loot
41 Jacqueline in *The Deep*
42 Furry scarfs
44 Winter slop
45 Candelabra-shaped letters
46 Short break in the storm
47 Not ___ many words
48 Helvetica, for one
49 Billionth: Comb. form
50 Sports analyst Collinsworth
51 Contrary flow
53 "Luck ___ Lady"

★ Futoshiki

Fill in the 5 x 5 grid with the numbers from 1 to 5 once per row and column, while following the greater than/lesser than symbols shown. There is only one valid solution that can be reached through logic and clear thinking alone!

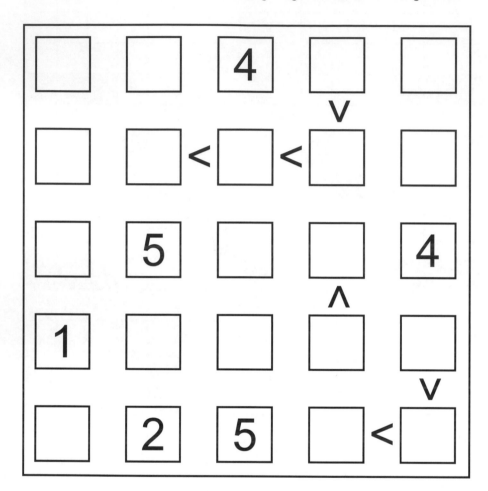

LETTERBLOCKS

Move the letterblocks around so that words are formed on top and below that you can associate with construction. In some blocks, the letter from the top row has been switched with the letter from the bottom row.

O	N	P	E	E	R	M
L	R	F	M	A	U	B

★ BrainSnack®—Veg Choice

Which vegetable (1–5) should replace the question mark?

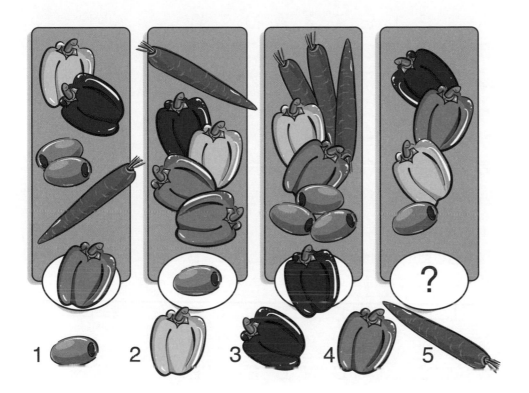

QUICK CROSSWORD

Place the words listed below in the crossword grid.

ALT ALTO BLUES GIG GROUPIE JAZZ JIG LEAD PAD RIG SALSA SOUL SPIN

★ Pizza

All the words are hidden vertically, horizontally or diagonally—in both directions. The letters that remain unused form a sentence from left to right.

```
I M A L A S P I E Z Z A M T W
R O U N D A S Y O K O R O U I
E G N T S U R C E V A M Z C L
C I A N A L L Y E A A B Z I I
E N P N M V E N S T S N A T O
I L O C C O R B O E E T R D I
P N L N A H O A S P V L E E C
S D I I T P O R O B A I L S A
L O T U N A E V H R R Y L U L
A O P N P P D R I S D E A O Z
O F T A P I H E S E U E H I O
N A D E R I N S H H S M R C N
A E P A S M S E I D N C E I E
G S B E C O E M A S O E P L O
E P L I S A B S A P U U L E A
R R I I N M A L A N P Y G D P
O A R T C S T O F N T L H H E
W O R T A E L F R E E Z E R D
```

DOUGH
EAT
FREEZER
HERBS
MOZZARELLA
MUSHROOM
NAPOLI
OIL
OLIVES
ORDER
OREGANO
OVEN
PARMESAN
PEPPER
PIECE
PINEAPPLE
ROUND
SALAMI
SALT
SEAFOOD
SLICE
TOMATO
TUNA
YEAST

ANCHOVIES   BROCCOLI   CRUST
BAKE   CALZONE   CUT
BASIL   CAPERS   DELICIOUS

DELETE ONE

Delete one letter from WINTERY LOFT and scoop up a prize.

★ Broadway Musicals II by Linda Lather

ACROSS

1 Undercover operative
5 Beguine, e.g.
10 Air Force installation
14 Locale of an ancient garden
15 Bagel flavoring
16 Freed or Cranston
17 "Temptation" musical
20 Hem and haw
21 Lansbury of stage and screen
22 The Lion King heroine
23 Betting money
24 Knight's defense
27 Family tree member
31 Maguire in Spider-Man
32 Piano factory employee
33 Cry's partner
34 Humdinger
35 Stringent
36 Speck of dust
37 Mrs. Eddie Cantor
38 Zellweger of Jerry Maguire
39 Did a shoe repair
40 Richard Rodgers, notably
42 Punters on the Thames
43 Famous cookie man
44 Second
45 Biblical book I or II
48 Distribute
52 "Edelweiss" musical
54 Cullen family matriarch
55 Macbeth or Macduff
56 Dryer trap stuff
57 "___ Indigo"
58 Eddie Munster's snake
59 Greek war goddess

DOWN

1 Synchronize
2 Garfield beagle
3 Something to shoot through
4 Call the shots
5 Daisy Duck's beau
6 Santa ___ Derby
7 Lowest card in pinochle
8 Simple bed
9 Made improvements
10 Party boats
11 Side petals
12 Go to sea
13 Resort SE of Palermo
18 Leghorn's land
19 PC command
23 "It's the Hard-Knock Life" musical
24 Even-keeled
25 John Wayne western
26 Steel bar
27 Cousin of a gimlet
28 Oarlock pin
29 Remote
30 Clarinet and oboe
32 Rake prongs
35 Steadfast
36 Minute particle
38 Star-crossed lover
39 Biblical sin city
41 Hesitated
42 Rob
44 Solitary
45 Ski turn
46 "I see!"
47 Post-it message
48 Golfer Scott
49 X ___ xylophone
50 Lilliputian
51 "Ghostbusters" car
53 Tampa Bay Lightning org.

★ Spot the Differences

Find the nine differences in the image on the right.

DOUBLETALK

Homophones are words that share the same pronunciation, no matter how they are spelled. If they are spelled differently then they are called heterographs. Find heterographs meaning:

LARGE BUILDING and PULL

★ Sudoku X

Fill in the grid so that each row, each column and each 3 x 3 frame contains every number from 1 to 9. The two main diagonals of the grid also contain every number from 1 to 9.

7	1			5			2	
8	2					6		
6	5	9	8	2			3	
	3	5	6	7		8		1
1				4		2		
2			3				4	
		6		9	7			
			2					
				3				

BLOCK ANAGRAM

Form the word that is described in the brackets with the letters above the grid. An extra letter is already in the right place.

MIDSTREAM (someone who has exceptional intellectual ability)

							N	

★ Similar Starts by Fran Canfield

ACROSS

1 Brother hood
5 Cow
10 "Excuse me, but ..."
14 Canton locale
15 Some cobblers of lore
16 Eggplant color
17 Cooperstown attraction
19 Chug along
20 Stoats
21 Black and white board game
23 Touch up
24 Fifth person
25 General assistant
27 Grave
30 Admonition to a cinema gabber
33 Rightful
35 Exploit
36 "Take ___ from me"
38 Capital of Morocco
40 Spanish 101 pronoun
41 The Dark Knight director
43 Dunking item
45 Hyperbolic timespan
46 Milk measures
48 Ocho minus cinco
50 Cuba libre ingredient
51 Quiz show fodder
55 ___ the Wanderer (gothic novel)
58 Ardent
59 Et ___ (and others)
60 Rowdy one
62 Trace the shape of
63 Dijon darling
64 King's term of address
65 Mexican gray wolf
66 Top Fuel fuel
67 Major addition

DOWN

1 "Suzanne" songwriter Leonard
2 United Airlines hub
3 One of the Flintstones
4 Humbert Humbert's passion
5 Guardian
6 Landon and Kjellin
7 School founded by T. Jefferson
8 Pixar clownfish
9 Dangerous fly
10 A glutton has a big one
11 Jane Addams's settlement
12 Bionomics: Abbr.
13 "Love ___": Beatles
18 Baseball pioneer Buck
22 His and ___
26 "Yikes!"
27 Handwriting feature
28 Golden Rule preposition
29 Ipkiss in The Mask
30 Belted out
31 Colonnade for Zeno
32 Pikes Peak race
34 Blood system
37 Mr. Ed, for one
39 John in Anger Management
42 ___ contendere
44 Land in ancient Rome
47 Detroit from New York
49 Gary in Forrest Gump
52 Social call
53 Like helium, chemically
54 Concur
55 Retail complex
56 Italian novelist Vittorini
57 Chrysler engine
58 Fog up
61 Sodom escapee

★★ BrainSnack®—Letter Pairs

Which letterblock completes the series?

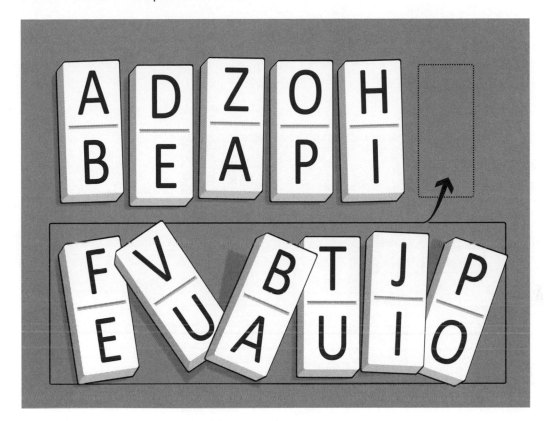

QUICK WORD SEARCH

Find the words related to television listed below in the word search grid.

```
N E E R C S E D I W E L B A C
R E L L I R H T S A R T N O C
E M I T B R O A D C A S T B X
J N Y E U G O L A N A M A R D
E T I B D N U O S G N I T A R
```

ABC LINE LOG SOUNDBITE WIDESCREEN SCREEN ANALOG BOX
CONTRAST TIME CABLE DUB BROADCAST RATINGS DRAMA THRILLER ART

★ Kakuro

Each number in a black area is the sum of the numbers that you have to enter in the next empty boxes. The empty boxes that make up the sum are called a run. The sum of the across run is written above the diagonal in the black area and the sum of the down run is written below the diagonal. Runs can only contain the numbers 1 through 9 and each number in a run can only be used once. The gray boxes only contain odd numbers and the white only even numbers.

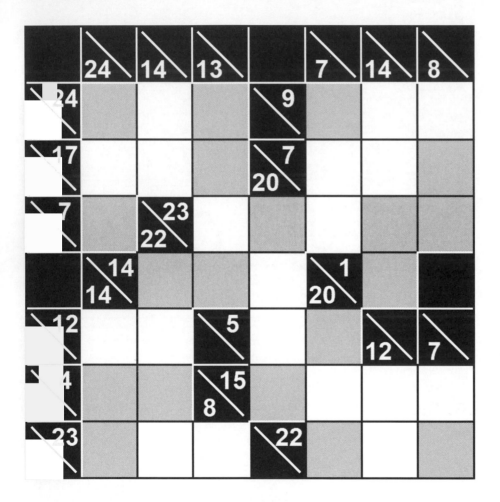

DOUBLETALK

Homophones are words that share the same pronunciation, no matter how they are spelled. If they are spelled differently then they are called heterographs. Find heterographs meaning:

PART OF A ROOM and SECURING

★ Similar Endings by Fran Canfield

ACROSS

1 Diane of *Numb3rs*
5 Decided collectively
10 Model Heming
14 Succulent plant
15 Place for a French lesson
16 Dove sounds
17 Historic Boston neighborhood
19 Fill the hold
20 White weasels
21 Bereft of trappings
23 Coach's list
24 "Agreed!"
25 Precambrian and others
27 Came to a boil
30 Ecclesiastic robe
33 Plunge in
35 Separate by sifting
36 Hundred-Acre-Wood denizen
38 Howe who knew how to sew
40 Hunk of dirt
41 Fix
43 Atomizer mist
45 Liberace's nickname
46 1995 Sydney Pollack film
48 Like past mistakes
50 Days long gone
51 Meditative exercise
55 Perform successfully
58 Gets cozy
59 Subject word
60 London venue of the BBC Proms
62 Scrabble piece
63 Matt in *The Bourne Supremacy*
64 One of the Great Lakes
65 Shakespeare title opener
66 Flared dress style
67 Model T rivals

DOWN

1 Company of pencil pushers?
2 2004 Oldsmobile model
3 Gallivants
4 Narrate
5 Hold in esteem
6 "Bound for Glory" singer Phil
7 You, to Yvette
8 Raines or Grasso
9 Mislead
10 On cloud nine
11 1980 horror comedy film
12 Boggy area
13 "___ forgive those who ..."
18 Unique people
22 Answers a raise
26 Puerto Rican dance
27 "Photograph" singer
28 Bacchanal cry
29 "___ Dinah": Frankie Avalon
30 Greystoke's foster parents
31 Broad-topped hill
32 Hall-of-Fame Black Hawk
34 Famous oversleeper
37 Batgirl and Wonder Woman
39 White wine
42 Dismal
44 Quick bread's lack
47 State admitted during the Civil War
49 State of flustered excitement
52 County north of Limerick
53 Indy winner Castroneves
54 Kahoolawe et al.
55 NYC-based theater org.
56 Slinky shape
57 JFK-to-TLV carrier
58 Caesars Palace sign
61 Adele is a member of this

★ Sudoku Twin

Fill in the grid so that each row, each column and each 3 x 3 frame contains every number from 1 to 9. A sudoku twin is two connected 9 x 9 sudokus.

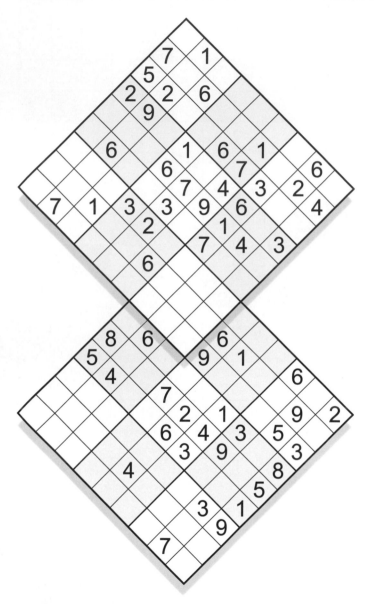

TRIANAGRAM

Three-word groups of anagrams are also called triplets or trianagrams.
Complete the group:

DEMAND   _ _ _ _ _ _   _ _ _ _ _ _

★ Hourglass

Starting in the middle, each word in the top half has the letters of the word below it, plus a new letter, and each word in the bottom half has the letters of the word above it, plus a new letter.

(1) someone who prowls or sneaks about
(2) athlete
(3) put at risk
(4) carry out

(5) baked dessert
(6) make a screeching noise
(7) used to strike a ball
(8) hunter

SANDWICH

What four-letter word belongs between the word on the left and the word on the right, so that the first and second word, and the second and third word, each form a common compound word or phrase?

C L O C K _ _ _ _ S H Y

★ Primate Puzzle by Tim Wagner

ACROSS

1 Rowling's Beedle, e.g.
5 *The Bell Jar* novelist
10 Ruler over Tolstoy
14 Melville book
15 Mr. Moto player
16 Cronyn in *Cocoon*
17 Muscat locale
18 *Surfing the Zeitgeist* writer
19 Enthusiastic vigor
20 Cutting up
23 Philanthropist Lilly
24 *The Cyberiad* author Stanislaw
25 Lighthearted
29 Quickly and quietly, e.g.
33 "Look at me, ___ helpless ..."
34 "Ugh!"
36 In place
37 *Sesame Street* network
38 Old English letter
39 Act like a baby
40 Jacutinga and tinstone
42 It's a start
44 Provoke
45 Skulking coward
47 Absolute quiet
49 French Open winner Ivanovic
50 Place for a school dance
51 Pierre Boulle novel
60 Cargo bay
61 Like argon or krypton
62 "Sock___ me!"
63 "Cleopatre" artist
64 Jenny's *Love Story* love
65 Zola femme fatale
66 Wash and ___
67 Chute material
68 ___-Pei dog

DOWN

1 Rapid expansion
2 BBs
3 Colorful mount
4 Mommies of hinnies
5 In theaters
6 City in California or Wisconsin
7 Galway Bay islands
8 High school math
9 Announces with fanfare
10 1976 Gregory Peck film
11 *Enterprise* officer
12 ___ *for All Seasons* (1966)
13 Separate forcefully
21 New Hampshire river
22 Gun the engine
25 Two-legged rifle mount
26 Eclipse shadow
27 Mirages, at times
28 Dernier cri
29 Campfire residue
30 Patrol mission
31 Containing element #56
32 Fashion
35 Takes too many pills
41 Lionel of *Hart to Hart*
42 Public speech
43 Screw in
44 Stays on
46 Brittany burro
48 Sodium hydroxide
51 "Close shave!"
52 Tribal knowledge
53 Edmonton locale: Abbr.
54 Part of ROM
55 Backslid
56 ZZ Top, for one
57 Tut's "divine potter"
58 Volcano near Messina
59 Fly like an eagle

★★★ Sport Maze

Draw the shortest way from the ball to the goal. You can only move along vertical and horizontal lines, not along diagonal lines. The figure on each square indicates the number of squares the ball must be moved in the same direction. You can change direction at each stop.

●	2	4	1	3	5
4	3	1	4	4	1
1	3	2	2	3	3
1	3	3	3	4	2
3	1	4	4	4	5
4	5	2	4	3	3

ONE LETTER LESS OR MORE

The word on the right side contains the letters of the word on the left side plus or minus the letter in the middle. One letter is already in the right place.

R U D E N E S S -E- U ☐ ☐ ☐ ☐ ☐ ☐

★ BrainSnack®—Shape Shifter

Which group of elements (1–6) does not belong?

DOODLE PUZZLE

A doodle puzzle is a combination of images, letters and/or numbers that represent a word or a concept. If you cannot solve a doodle puzzle, do not look at the answer right away. Think hard—and outside the box.

★ 2012 Ryder Cup by John M. Samson

ACROSS

1 Crook by Hook
5 Place for pumpkins
10 Oil-rich nation
14 Tupper of Tupperware
15 Sunny lobbies
16 Elihu for whom an Ivy is named
17 2012 Ryder Cup golfer
19 Spartan portico
20 Not neat
21 Self-conscious giggle
23 Red Wings great Sid
24 Jacobi in *I, Claudius*
25 Like a river delta
28 Impoverished
31 Unusual partner?
32 Bags with handles
33 Track rival of Ovett
34 Pre-Derby filly race
35 Took part in a regatta
36 "___ is so sudden!"
37 Salt Lake player
38 First Egyptian king
39 "Veni, vidi, vici," e.g.
40 Rio's "Christ the ___"
42 Jim in *The Mask*
43 Horse opera
44 "___ Buy Me Love": Beatles
45 Slightly colored
47 Capital of Chile
51 Suffix with poet
52 2012 Ryder Cup golfer
54 Unusual breathing noise
55 Acclimate
56 Advanced
57 Draws to a close
58 "Danseuse" artist
59 Picnic crashers

DOWN

1 Firms up
2 "You've got ___" (AOL message)
3 Therefore
4 Takes higher
5 Hocked
6 Coral reef
7 *Iliad* setting
8 Valencia conqueror
9 Made tracks
10 Bluepoint
11 2012 Ryder Cup golfer
12 Ubiquitous medicinal plant
13 Within shouting distance
18 Gray soldier
22 Gets to
24 Sees socially
25 Search high and low
26 Howling mad
27 2012 Ryder Cup golfer
28 Secluded arbor
29 Press secretary's asset
30 Out of sorts
32 Pore-shrinking lotion
35 Corrected
36 Burrito wrap
38 Allocate (out)
39 African language family
41 "Witchy Woman" group
42 Birchbarks
44 *Platinum Blonde* director
45 Radial or retread
46 Empowering motto
47 Like a rugged bug?
48 Akhenaton's god
49 Guy
50 Repast remnants
53 Scottish one

★ Walt Disney

All the words are hidden vertically, horizontally or diagonally—in both directions. The letters that remain unused form a sentence from left to right.

```
K W A L T K C A B H C N U H D
O B M U D I M Y D A L S N C E
O Y H E R C U L E S C R R T E
B P M A R T L N A Z R A T I A
E P F T E N A D S Y D E H T C
L I A S E A N S I T O B E S I
G N N A T P I T T U N R L A N
N O T T I R D A N A O E I L D
U C A N H E D C A E L H O D E
J C S O W T A O L B I T N D R
L H I H W E L T T G V O K U E
C I A A O P A S A N E R I K L
S O L C N E V I E I R B N N L
Y E A O S R S R A P F T G E A
C O P P E R E A M E R L I N R
H C R E A L T E I E G O O F Y
I N G M A I C H A L I C E K E
P Y M D O U S T E S I B M A B
```

DUMBO
FANTASIA
GOOFY
HERCULES
HUNCHBACK
JUNGLE BOOK
LADY
LILO
MERLIN
MULAN
OLIVER
PETER PAN
PINOCCHIO
POCAHONTAS
SLEEPING BEAUTY
SNOW WHITE
STITCH
TARZAN
THE ARISTOCATS
THE LION KING
TOD
TRAMP

ALADDIN
ALICE
ATLANTIS

BAMBI
BROTHER BEAR
CHIP

CINDERELLA
COPPER
DALE

FRIENDS?

What do the following words have in common?

LAND JACK BROW BALL FLYER LIFE SPOT

★ Word Sudoku

Complete the grid so that each row, each column and each 3 x 3 frame contains the nine letters from the black box below. The hidden nine-letter word is in the diagonal from top left to bottom right.

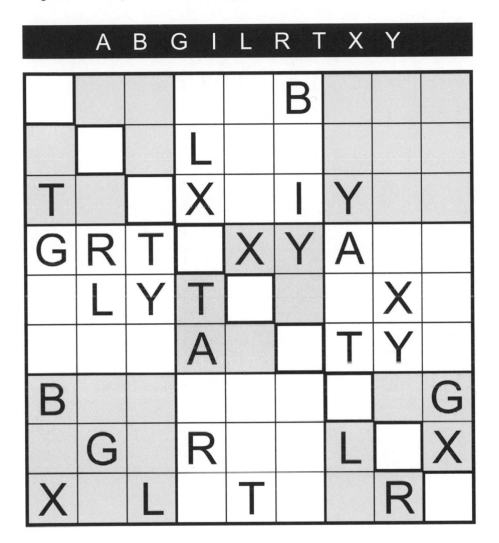

A B G I L R T X Y

UNCANNY TURN

Rearrange the letters of the phrase below to form a cognate anagram, one which is related or connected in meaning to the original phrase. The answer can be one or more words.

BECAME FAT CURIO

★ Binairo

Complete the grid with zeros and ones until there are 6 zeros and 6 ones in every row and every column. No more than two of the same number can be next to or under each other. Rows or columns with exactly the same content are not allowed. There is only one valid solution.

					I		O				
	O						I		I	I	
			O		I						I
	O						I		O		
		I			O						
							O		I		
I		I		O		I		O	O		O
						O					O
	O		O		O		I		O	O
O				I						
					O					O	O

CHANGELINGS

Each of the three lines of letters below spell words that have a connection with books, but the letters have been mixed up. Four letters from the first word are now in the third line, four letters from the third word are in the second line and four letters from the second word are in the first line. The remaining letters are in their original places. What are the words?

B S T A L O N R S T
H E C T S E T L E E
C A A R A N G I R S

★★ Independence by Peggy O'Shea

ACROSS

1 Sow's spouse
5 Send to another club
10 Amberjack's cousin
14 Piece of the farm
15 Brought in
16 Sushi fish
17 New York Harbor sight
20 Old ones die hard, they say
21 Plato's teacher
22 Hayworth of film
24 Plane for quick takeoffs
25 Weather Channel guess
29 Minis/maxis
33 Center or cycle opener
34 Playful prank
36 Become used to
37 "Angels in the Snow" pianist
39 *Alice in Wonderland* cat
41 Tingling
42 Religion
44 Update boundaries
46 Halloween, for one
47 Globetrotter's home
49 Insisted
51 Red herring, e.g.
53 Prefix for present
54 Gym dandies?
58 Some regatta teams
62 1965 civil-rights demonstrators
64 Mannered behavior
65 *Somewhere in Time* star
66 1982 Jeff Bridges film
67 Legendary seamstress
68 "Slammin' Sammy" of golf
69 Exercise units

DOWN

1 Whoop-de-do
2 Twice tetra-
3 Kaffiyeh wearer
4 Sack out
5 Stephen King novel
6 2016 Olympics city
7 Basset sounds
8 Cyclades island
9 Pronouncements
10 Thievery
11 Brusque
12 Feed the kitty
13 Calendar squares
18 Central New York city
19 Busted
23 No longer sleeping
25 Canine command
26 *The Magic Flute* is one
27 Flight section
28 Like a fork or a trident
30 Like composition paper
31 Treasure stash
32 Gave a darn?
35 Relief carving
38 Like newborns
40 Hit the nail on the head
43 Took a line out
45 Stampede stimulus
48 Takes the roadster out
50 Work shift for some
52 Sana'a is its capital
54 At a distance
55 Certain chamber group
56 Not his
57 Hook's underling
59 Roll response
60 Compete in the Breeders Crown
61 Nine-digit IDs
63 Palindromic name

★ Horoscope

Fill in the grid so that every row, every column and every frame of six boxes contains six different symbols: health, work, money, happiness, family and love. Look at the row or column that corresponds with your sign of the zodiac and find out which of the six symbols are important for you today. The symbols appear in increasing order of importance (1–6). It's up to you to translate the meaning of each symbol to your specific situation.

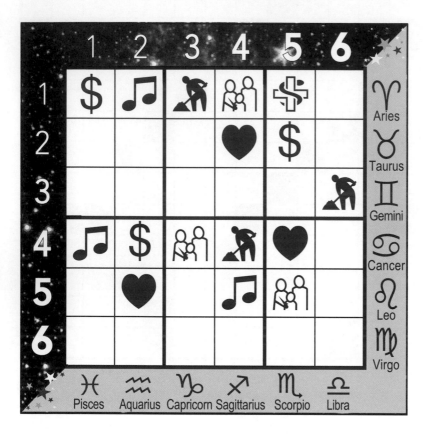

WORD WALL

Beginning at the left side of the wall, make a word by adding one group of letters from each column as you move left to right. When you have found the first word, go back to the second column and start the next word, gathering one group of letters from each column, and so on until all the letters are used to make six words.

★★ BrainSnack®—Twinkle Twinkle

Which star doesn't belong in the sky?

SYMBOL SUMS

Can you work out these number sums using three of these four symbols? **＋ － ÷ ×**
(No fractions or minus numbers are involved in the sum as you progress from left to right.)

12 ☐ 3 ☐ 4 ☐ 12 = 4

★★ Longings by Teresa Lucchetti

ACROSS

1 Safe place for a boat
5 Carnival dances
11 Arabic robe
14 Mine approach
15 Seasick
16 Seek office
17 It's done at Trevi Fountain
20 Poked along
21 *I-Ching* readers
22 Langley initials
23 Brings about, biblical style
24 Sound from a zebra?
28 Squire in *Silas Marner*
30 It may be tossed in a ring
31 Druggist's weight
33 Pre-remote channel changer
37 Player of Obi-Wan
39 Pride Lands dwellers
40 Husband
41 Note from the boss
42 Conductor Klemperer
43 Fisherman's profit?
44 Memphis deity
46 Planet that Triton orbits
50 Mown-down strip
53 Slangy turndown
54 Sicily's capital
57 Vitamin found in beef liver
61 Tennessee Williams play (with 67-A)
63 Suburban trailer?
64 All in one piece
65 Unexpected delay
66 Biblical father of Abner
67 See 61 Across
68 Warsaw resident

DOWN

1 Crow cries
2 Norse god of war
3 MasterCard rival
4 Law school subject
5 Piglet sound
6 "___ Lang Syne"
7 Saw face-to-face
8 Thai money
9 Argento in *Marie Antoinette*
10 Religious councils
11 Start one's day
12 Diamond sacrifices
13 Feeling for Woody Allen
18 Pass quickly
19 Mall stalls
24 "Kapow!"
25 Healthy
26 Bullet on an agenda
27 Cabaret singer Piaf
28 Copier maker
29 Mornings
32 "Rubbish!"
34 Part of Mork's sign-off
35 "Hansel and Gretel" prop
36 ___ noire
38 Eggbeater
39 Mauna ___
45 Kind of movie glasses
47 Steak au poivre, e.g.
48 En-passant capture
49 *Little Orphan Annie* character
50 2010 World Cup champion
51 Fritter away
52 Change the fit
55 Biblical wall word
56 Baseball's Mel and Ed
57 Comedienne Roseanne
58 K-P connectors
59 Osso buco meat
60 Ford SUV
62 LI doubled

★★★ Sudoku

Fill in the grid so that each row, each column and each 3 x 3 frame contains every number from 1 to 9.

9			7				3	
8	7	2	3		4	1		
			8		5		9	4
2	1	5	9		3	4	7	6
			5	7	1			
								1
						9	1	3
		9	6				8	
				3				

TRIANAGRAM

Three-word groups of anagrams are called triplets or trianagrams.
Complete the group:

S N I P E   _ _ _ _ _   _ _ _ _ _

★★ Number Cluster

Complete the grid by constituting adjoining clusters that consist of as many cubes as the number on the cubes. At cube 5, for instance, you will have to make a five-cube cluster. Two or more figure cubes of the same value belong to the same cluster. You can only place your cubes along horizontal and/or vertical lines.

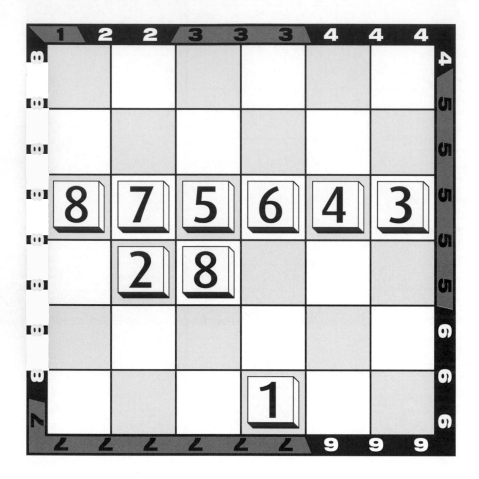

CHANGELINGS

Each of the three lines of letters below spell words that have a connection with art, but the letters have been mixed up. Four letters from the first word are now in the third line, four letters from the third word are in the second line and four letters from the second word are in the first line. The remaining letters are in their original places. What are the words?

X A B N T B T U S N

E L H I D I C I O E

P A N I S R A P H S

★★ From the Heart by Cindy Wheeler

ACROSS

1 "Wish you ___ here!"
5 Jilts
10 Land plan
14 Lod Airport carrier
15 *The Mill on the Floss* author
16 *Mazes and Monsters* author Jaffe
17 1968 hit for the Troggs
20 Apparition
21 Opposing forces
22 "___ Skelter": Beatles
23 *Family Guy* mom
24 Vermin
26 Handel work
29 *Damn Yankees* vamp
32 Err
34 Icicle locale
35 Suffix for lemon
36 Novelist Rand
37 San Francisco hill
38 Wharf
40 Cry uncle
42 Postal sheet
43 Harvest goddess
45 Former city near Tokyo
47 Ottoman VIP
48 "The Raven" maiden
52 Tia in *Wayne's World*
55 Despised
56 1955 Frank Sinatra hit
58 "I'm working ___"
59 Infer from data
60 Flaherty's "Man of ___"
61 Man caves
62 Wives of knights
63 Beer holders

DOWN

1 Swansea citizens
2 Slip off to tie a knot
3 Frazzle
4 Carmen in *Disaster Movie*
5 Abandons
6 Gland ending
7 Wire measure
8 Indy 500 position
9 Erle ___ Gardner
10 Word of honor
11 Pelican State
12 "Snowbird" singer Murray
13 Little ones
18 Willow genus
19 Flying Cloud and Speed Wagon
25 Companionway
26 Virile
27 Bath's river
28 Cupbearer to the gods
29 Columbo's employer
30 Jon Arbuckle's dog
31 *Cat Ballou* star
33 Reuben bread
39 "Miss Otis ___": Cole Porter
40 Had quite an itch
41 Hogwarts teacher Umbridge
42 Famed Ottawa chief
44 "Take ___ Train"
46 Neighboring
49 *Gone With the Wind* heroine
50 Cordelia's sister
51 Unspoiled locales
52 Lunkhead
53 First-rate
54 Early Icelandic epic
55 Needlepoint fabric
57 Not saying a word

★★ Concentration—Lateral Thinking

Connect the sixteen dots with one continuous line. You can only change direction five times.

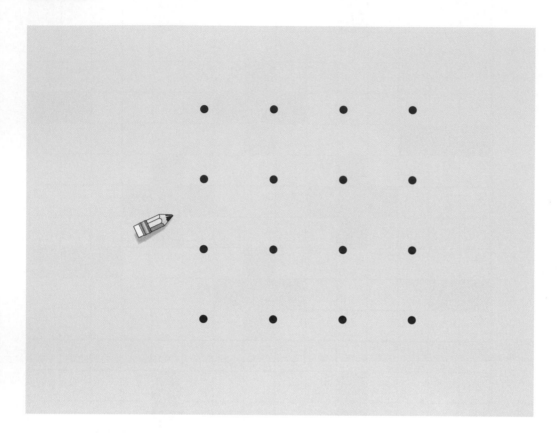

LETTER LINE

Put a letter in each of the squares below to make a word that means "relationship." The number clues refer to other words which can be made from the whole.

4 1 2 6 2 WATERING HOLE; 5 10 9 11 2 LOOSE CHANGE;
5 1 2 9 11 10 GAMBLING HOUSE; 1 5 8 9 4 11 DEED;
5 4 1 2 8 EDGE

1	2	3	4	5	6	7	8	9	10	11

★ BrainSnack®—Color Palette

Which paint (1–3) was used the most to color in the three shapes?

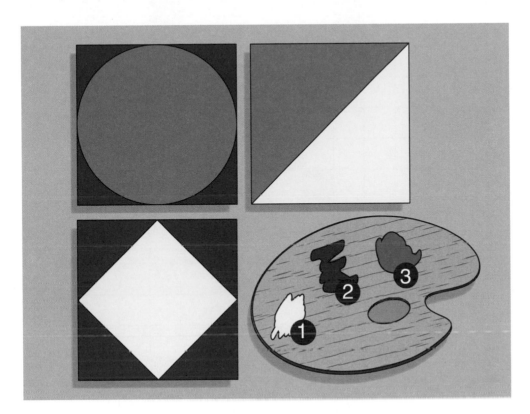

CLOCKWISE

The answers to the clues from 1 to 12 are all seven-letter words that end with the letter M. When you have solved the puzzle correctly, working clockwise from 1, the twelve letters in the outer circle will spell a word meaning "underground."

1 Geological layer
2 Unchanging or identical
3 To come to a peak in development
4 Place name
5 Catchy tune (inf.)
6 Practical acceptance of the facts
7 Public speaker's platform
8 Presidential first name
9 Ad—(to an excessive, tiresome degree)
10 Pointed, witty, concise remark
11 Word with opposite meaning
12 Quack medicine

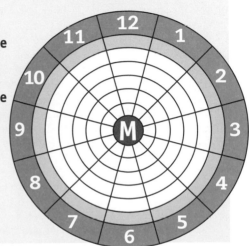

★★ Angelina Jolie by Brian O'Shea

ACROSS

1 Utah ski spot
5 Stingy person
10 Airline to Ben-Gurion
14 River to the Rhine
15 Ekberg in *La Dolce Vita*
16 Bering Air hub
17 Epithet of Athena
18 1999 Angelina Jolie film
20 Boning pros
22 Took for the summer, maybe
23 Midway Airport alternative
24 Eschew humility
25 High-spirited
27 Looks after
31 Goosebump-causing
32 Some circus performers
33 Question about process
34 Waterless
35 Sprung
36 Indira's gown
37 NFL stats
38 Antiseptic
39 Is dog-tired?
40 In the open air
42 Scows
43 It follows soft or silver
44 Playground sight
45 Unruffled
48 "Yellow Rose of Texas" city
51 1997 Angelina Jolie film
53 Vardalos and Peeples
54 One kind of oil
55 "Chain Gang" singer
56 *Lost ___ Mancha* (2002)
57 Queen Mary II's successor
58 Sea eagles
59 John in *King Kong*

DOWN

1 Horse for Lawrence
2 Remarkable sort
3 2010 Angelina Jolie film
4 Spider, e.g.
5 Flimsy
6 Grow accustomed to
7 Pay lip service to?
8 Biblical suffix
9 System with a track record?
10 Mesh gears
11 Development subdivisions
12 Gaston's gal pal
13 Libraries do it
19 ___-foot-oil
21 Codlike fish
24 Alien race in *Deep Space Nine*

25 "From ___ shining ..."
26 Hidden
27 Prayers
28 2008 Angelina Jolie film
29 Flourless cake
30 ___ chard
32 "___ Jacques"
35 Where to find the Ponte Vecchio
36 Italian island
38 South American animal with a snout
39 Unexciting poker hand
41 ___ Johnson (The Rock)
42 Ruben in *Disorganized Crime*
44 Sign of an engine problem
45 Adoption agcy.

46 PayPal founder Musk
47 Apply the needle and thread
48 Balanchine ballet
49 Ashlee Simpson song
50 Sandy ridges
52 "Blimey!"

★ Printing

All the words are hidden vertically, horizontally or diagonally—in both directions. The letters that remain unused form a sentence from left to right.

```
K T H Q U I C K D R Y I N G E
P O P L A T N Q F H E N P R E
E A O S S I U I P R O O F N V
I S G B T I L A H E O L D E I
E S T E R M R C S O F F S E T
T Y P E E G O O F L P R I R A
C U S T O M E R S M E N T C G
I N G H P R P R E A E B S S E
S T T U E H E P A R N P A K N
E I T B R E I S P G G R E L D
L E B S E S T E D I R O N I A
R U T O T G H S E N A F D S E
R O E N I Z A G A M V O R R L
M T W A U T O M A T I C I T Y
N O I T A R U G I F N O C H T
H H E H E L L A T I G I D P O
F P A P L A M A T E R I A L S
S D R A C S S E N I S U B T E
```

FILM
IMAGE
INK
LABELS
LEAD
LITHOGRAPHY
MAGAZINE
MARGIN
MATERIALS
NEGATIVE
OFFSET
PAGE
PHOTO
PROOF
QUICK-DRYING
QUIRE
RUBBER
SHEETS
SILK-SCREEN

AUTOMATIC
BOOK
BUSINESS CARDS

COMPUTER
CONFIGURATION
CUSTOMERS

DIGITAL
DRY
ENGRAVING

DELETE ONE

Delete one letter from MANLY AS IF FATE and let your imagination run wild.

★ Futoshiki

Fill in the 5 x 5 grid with the numbers from 1 to 5 once per row and column, while following the greater than/lesser than symbols shown. There is only one valid solution that can be reached through logic and clear thinking alone!

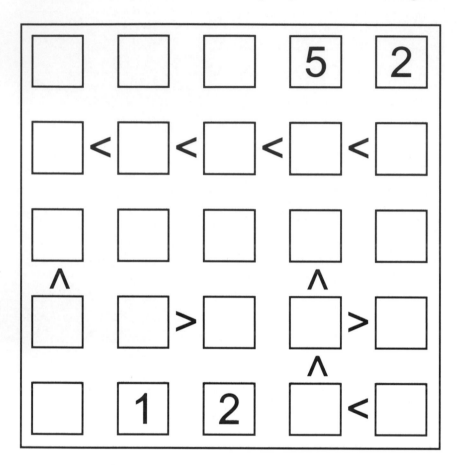

SYMBOL SUMS

Can you work out these number sums using three of these four symbols? **+ − ÷ ×**
(No fractions or minus numbers are involved in the sum as you progress from left to right.)

$$7 \; \square \; 2 \; \square \; 1 \; \square \; 4 = 20$$

★★ Alec Baldwin by Peggy O'Shea

ACROSS

1 Governess to King Mongkut's brood
5 Tear to bits
10 Lid issue
14 Beer feature
15 Liqueur flavor
16 Mess-hall serving
17 2004 Alec Baldwin film
19 "I'm outa ___!"
20 Cox of *St. Elsewhere*
21 File holder
23 Took a round trip?
26 Conical dwelling
27 Antenna or tentacle
28 Summarized
31 Province
32 Wharf space
33 Foolhardy goddess
34 Interested in
35 Farsighted ones
36 Get ready
37 "___ Blu, Dipinto Di Blu"
38 Home of Romeo and Juliet
39 Subway
40 Unseen troublemakers
42 Mole or vole
43 Wiggly dessert
44 Happens to, as if by fate
45 Golf layout
47 Old stringed instrument
48 "Nine, ten, ___ fat hen"
49 1994 Alec Baldwin film
54 Little parasites
55 Wreck on the road
56 Gaucho weapon
57 Look of questionable intent
58 Jesse of Olympic fame
59 Make thoroughly wet

DOWN

1 Propeller's locale
2 Japanese theatrical style
3 Highlands turndown
4 Texas Panhandle city
5 Luise in *The Good Earth*
6 ___ *Out* (Kevin Kline film)
7 Weep for
8 *For the Boys* org.
9 Improves to the max
10 Haul, slangily
11 2006 Alec Baldwin film
12 Days of old
13 Still-life pitcher
18 Pulled a lever, maybe
22 Brightly hued fish
23 In the ___ (soon to come)
24 *Stand by Me* director
25 1988 Alec Baldwin film
26 *On the Waterfront* protagonist
28 Angling equipment
29 Everlasting, in odes
30 Stops on a line
32 Bingo relative
35 Very dangerous knife
36 Tricycle taxis
38 Tribulations
39 Choral work
41 Corporate union
42 Insurgents
44 Opened
45 "Safe!" or "Out!"
46 Off-Broadway award
47 Blood vessel network
50 In what manner?
51 Serenade
52 Chicken ___ reine
53 Lhasa beast

★★ Keep Going

Start on a blank square of your choice and connect as many blank squares as possible with one single continuous line. You can only connect squares along vertical and horizontal lines. You must continue the connecting line up until the next obstacle, i.e., the rim of the box, a black square or a square that has already been used. You can change direction at any obstacle you meet. Each square can be used only once. The number of blank squares that will be left unused is marked in the upper square. There is more than one solution. We show only one solution.

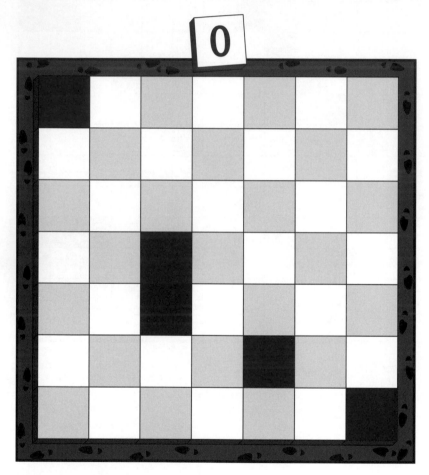

TRIANAGRAM

Three-word groups of anagrams are also called triplets or trianagrams.
Complete the group:

PARTS   _ _ _ _ _   _ _ _ _ _

★★★ Sport Maze

Draw the shortest way from the ball to the goal. You can only move along vertical and horizontal lines, not along diagonal lines. The figure on each square indicates the number of squares the ball must be moved in the same direction. You can change direction at each stop.

1	3	4	3	5	4
4	3	1	4	1	1
1	4	3	2	3	3
4	4	3	2	1	4
5	4	3	3	○	3
3	5	4	2	3	4

ONE LETTER LESS OR MORE

The word on the right side contains the letters of the word on the left side plus or minus the letter in the middle. One letter is already in the right place.

T R I A N G L E -L- _ R _ _ _ _ _

★★ Coast to Coast by Cindy Nell

ACROSS

1 Hamilton foe
5 Highway exits
10 Buckled
14 To ___ (just so)
15 Disney World park
16 Suffix for switch
17 Summer Olympics sport
20 Answered a job ad
21 One of the Twelve
22 Stubbs of *Sherlock*
23 "___ it there, pal!"
24 Support beam
28 Kix and Trix
32 Hydrant hook-on
33 Flavorable
35 Fume
36 *Enterprise* letters
37 Tattered cloth
38 Charles X, par exemple
39 One's bearing
41 Gillette razors
43 Patronize a restaurant
44 Unworthy of
46 Sit on
48 Web address
49 Speak lovingly
50 Former GM division
54 Assume
58 Place mentioned in "The Marines' Hymn"
60 Hogwarts librarian Pince
61 Bogart's *High Sierra* role
62 Liveliness
63 Blind a hawk
64 Greeted the judge
65 Bryan of Bon Jovi

DOWN

1 Rum cake
2 El Paso college
3 Use a sickle
4 No lover of company
5 Lets out
6 Footless creature
7 Middle of the 12th century
8 Negri in *Hi Diddle Diddle*
9 Like Mayan pyramids
10 Daniel or Noah
11 Part of QED
12 Winning coach of Super Bowl X
13 Painted tinware
18 Helpful information
19 "How Deep Is ___ Love": Bee Gees
24 Glove part
25 *The Manchurian Candidate* heroine
26 City on the Ruhr
27 Universal logo
28 Stogie
29 Eaglet's home
30 Musicians Redbone and Russell
31 Berlin's were blue
34 On a level
40 Unbiased
41 World books
42 Battened down
43 Took the plunge
45 Indy 500 winner Luyendyk
47 1969 Alan Arkin film
50 Electric flux symbols
51 Elbe tributary
52 Icy burg
53 Blazer
54 Battle of Normandy objective
55 *Return of the Jedi* dancer
56 Croat, e.g.
57 One, in Dresden
59 Away

★ BrainSnack®—Castle Conundrum

Which angle (1–5) of this castle is wrong?

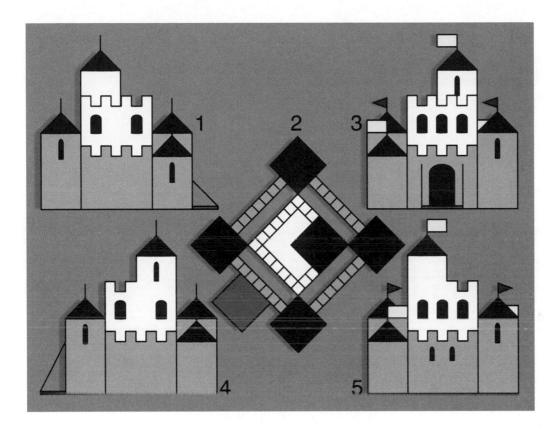

BLOCK ANAGRAM

Form the words that are described in the brackets with the letters above the grid. Extra letters are already in the right place.

CRISSCROSS POPE (hand game played by two)

| | | | K | | A | | | | | | | | | | R | |

★ Word Sudoku

Complete the grid so that each row, each column and each 3 x 3 frame contains the nine letters from the black box below. The hidden nine-letter word is in the diagonal from top left to bottom right.

A	H	I	M	N	O	R	T	Y

M				T			I	R
						A	O	N
Y	T		R					
O	M			I		N	T	
I			O		M			A
N				Y	R		A	
T						R	N	I
	R	O			T			Y

UNCANNY TURN

Rearrange the letters of the phrase below to form a cognate anagram, one which is related or connected in meaning to the original phrase. The answer can be one or more words.

ROOM IN TOP

★ Binairo

Complete the grid with zeros and ones until there are 5 zeros and 6 ones in every row and every column. No more than two of the same number can be next to or under each other. Rows or columns with exactly the same content are not allowed. There is only one valid solution.

					O					
					O					
		I		I	I				O	
		I		O				O	O	
O										
		O	O					O		
										I
		O				O		I		
			I	I						O
				O			O	O		O

SANDWICH

What five-letter word belongs between the word on the left and the word on the right, so that the first and second word, and the second and third word, each form a common compound word or phrase?

ABOVE _ _ _ _ _ ROOM

★★ Facial Features by Cindy Wheeler

ACROSS

1 Nun's skullcap
5 Vinegary
10 Prefix for sol
14 Sweet variety of tangelo
15 Lewis or Belafonte
16 Ibanez of baseball
17 *Watership Down* song
19 Manitoba Indian
20 Hippocampus
21 Glazed, as eyes
23 Some George Foreman wins
24 Madrid museum
25 Hordes
28 Like a lover, not a fighter
31 Large perennial
32 *Pocahontas* dog
33 Dernier ___ (latest fashion)
34 Electrical cord's end
35 Rapper's crew
36 Doubloon, for one
37 Caesar's language: Abbr.
38 Mountain ridge
39 Booted
40 Museum offerings
42 Basically
43 Work with weights
44 Physical injury
45 Melodious passage
47 Land with a small population?
51 Type of debt security
52 Pliers type
54 McCartney's ___ *Cor Meum*
55 Perfumer Lauder
56 Not landbound
57 It's for the birds
58 Chicken's place
59 Onion relative

DOWN

1 Tinker-Evers-Chance team
2 Brute of legend
3 Figure skater Kulik
4 Duking it out
5 Last team coached by Leo Durocher
6 Mating game
7 "Love, Me" singer Collin
8 Anger
9 Ignominy
10 Pinball palace
11 They're shucked and shocked
12 Has buyer's remorse
13 Composer Speaks
18 Contrived
22 Gossamer
24 As such
25 *The Giving Tree* tree
26 "Cool it!"
27 Lawyer, slangily
28 Flies, e.g.
29 Biblical archangel
30 Jitterbug cousin
32 Limerick men?
35 Joint occupant?
36 Record holder?
38 Vigoda and Beame
39 "Guitar Town" singer Steve
41 Pressed
42 Croquet stick
44 Doesn't want to be found
45 Heady brews
46 Risotto ingredient
47 Jared in *Urban Legend*
48 Emulate Kate Moss
49 Plaintiff
50 Sitar wood
53 Placido's "that"

★ Cage the Animals

Draw lines to completely divide up the grid into small squares with exactly one animal per square. The squares should not overlap.

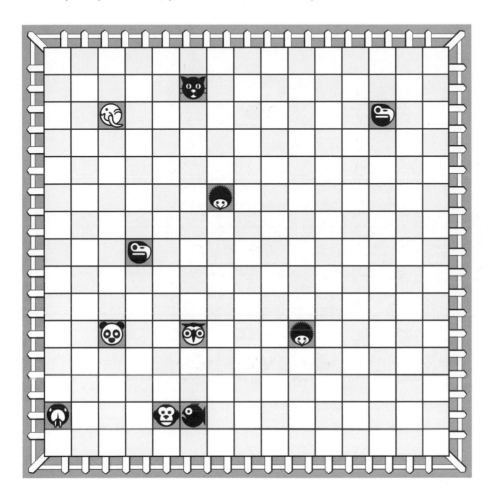

WORD WALL

Beginning at the left side of the wall, make a word by adding one group of letters from each column as you move left to right. When you have found the first word, go back to the second column and start the next word, gathering one group of letters from each column, and so on until all the letters are used to make six words.

★ BrainSnack®—Familiar Faces

Which figure (1–5) do you see most frequently three times in a row in all directions?

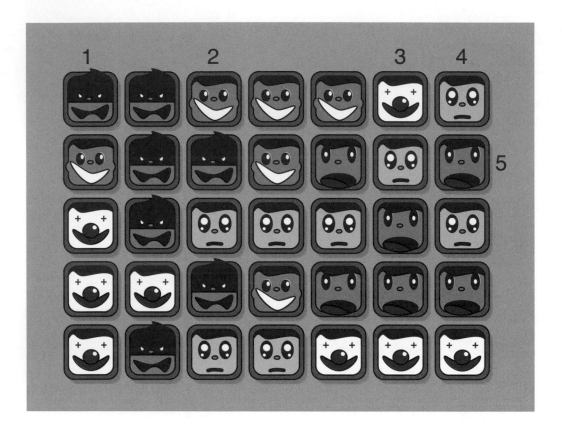

QUICK WORD SEARCH

Find the words related to vacations listed below in the word search grid.

TRIP CASE BALL FOOD STAY VILLA SWIM POOL TIME BIKE
FLY GUIDE HIKE JET PACK CARD AGENT WALK ZOO DRIVE TRAIN

★★ XXXs by Cindy Nell

ACROSS
1 Glided
5 Break down
10 "A likely story!"
14 Senator's gofer
15 *Invisible Cities* author Calvino
16 View from the pulpit
17 Bite-sized Hershey's candy
20 Airport event
21 Delighted
22 "Can't Help Lovin' ___ Man"
23 Black Sea naval base
24 Razed
28 "Orinoco Flow" singer
29 *Yale Daily News* staffers
30 *Staying Alive* music
32 Bruce in *Coming Home*
36 *Mad Men* network
37 Catch a bug
38 Caustic alkaline
39 Christmas
41 Open without a corkscrew
43 Deli salad
44 Heaping Pelion upon ___
46 Clan designs
48 Insightful
51 Negative link
52 Not fruitful
54 Squid cousin
58 Yard, slangily
60 Pentathlon sword
61 Secretive one
62 Whilom
63 Brooklyn team
64 Holy, to René
65 The Red and the Black

DOWN
1 Animal welfare gp.
2 *The Wizard of Oz* star
3 Marty's *Young Frankenstein* role
4 Gets off the fence
5 Expanded
6 Latin "and others"
7 Egyptian Mau, for one
8 Baldwin in *Beetlejuice*
9 She's heard on "Bungalow Bill"
10 As a proxy
11 Diamond thefts
12 Makes smooth
13 Seed coat
18 Ellipsoidal
19 Brickyard 400 site
24 Like good bacon
25 Seafarer's saint
26 Foible
27 "The Look of Love" singer Krall
28 Brilliant success
31 ___ semper tyrannis
33 Scat queen Fitzgerald
34 Jeri of *Body of Proof*
35 What anchors weigh
40 French pilgrimage town
41 Having no point
42 Griddlecake
43 Swings
45 Hubbub
47 Campus mil. training
48 Beyond pale
49 Dummy
50 Principle
53 Krabappel of *The Simpsons*
54 Sharif in *Hidalgo*
55 Dijon dad
56 Polaris bear
57 Concordes
59 Champagne adjective

★ Ball Sports

All the words are hidden vertically, horizontally or diagonally—in both directions. The letters that remain unused form a sentence from left to right.

```
B O W L I N G B A B O U N C E
D O D G E B A L L L L S W P O
S R T S O F T B A L L O F S T
C D A T H L E T E S R O A E R
O O R E D E F S C H O C K E Y
R R M A L O O P T T I C B T B
E E P P I R L B B D I I Y E A
L L I H E L E A A R N C B U S
B L T S O T L K C S H I G Q K
B A C A O L I I O R E N U O E
I B H U E C O T B O O B R R T
R D S Q E T C P I E N S A C B
D N X S T S D E R O T S S L A
L A O G A T I N R E N G F E L
R H O M T E U Q N A T E P H L
E M A T C H T N H P L A Y I R
D S E L T T I K S M I L W L E
N N I U M S B G N I L R U H C
```

DODGE BALL
DRIBBLE
FOOTBALL
GOAL
GOLF
HANDBALL
HOCKEY
HURLING
LACROSSE
MATCH
PETANQUE
PITCH
PLAY
POOL
RUGBY
SCORE
SKITTLES
SNOOKER
SOCCER
SOFTBALL
SQUASH
TENNIS
THROW
WATER POLO

ATHLETES
BASEBALL
BASKETBALL

BILLIARDS
BOUNCE
BOWLING

COMPETITION
CRICKET
CROQUET

DELETE ONE

Delete one letter from INCARNATE LOVE AD and find something nice in the mail.

★ Word Wheel

How many words of three or more letters, each including the letter at the center of the wheel, can you make from this diagram? No plurals or conjugations. We've found 20, including one nine-letter word. Can you do better?

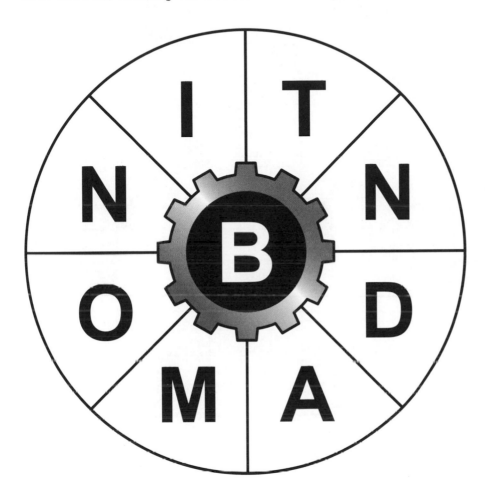

LETTERBLOCKS

Move the letterblocks around so that words are formed on top and below that you can associate with the body. In some blocks, the letter from the top row has been switched with the letter from the bottom row.

★★ **A Common Bond** by John M. Samson

ACROSS
1 Extra dry
5 Snail-mail item
10 Limburger quality
14 He loved Lucy
15 Gia Lam Airport location
16 Mama's mate
17 *For Your Eyes Only* author*
19 Level
20 Like the Dodger in *Oliver!*
21 Doing the driving
23 Prefix for derm or therm
25 Improved skills
26 Least likely to forgive
30 "Comme ci, comme ça!"
33 Fluffy scarf
34 Speak slowly
36 Cheap cigar
37 Is off-base
39 Berlin's were blue
41 Wanted soldier
42 Stop, at sea
44 Maestro Doráti
46 Elder Gershwin brother
47 Tropical wear
49 Continental
51 Soviet space dog
53 Google cofounder
54 Treat for the feet
57 Costly furs
61 64 Across, for one
62 What answers* have in common
64 "Dies ___"
65 Stealing: Prefix
66 Dalai ___
67 Let have for a while
68 Mattress name
69 Online publication, for short

DOWN
1 Sarah McLachlan hit
2 Be parental
3 Doesn't exist
4 Hold other views
5 Sanctuaries
6 Bagpiper's cap
7 Córdoba cordial
8 Billing cycle, often
9 Central Park bird
10 *Die Fledermaus,* for one
11 "Thursday's Child" singer*
12 Store sign
13 Jingled bells
18 Rational
22 Nephew of Abel
24 Honshu city
26 Tasman and Muzorewa
27 "Don't Know Why" singer Jones
28 *The Dark Knight Rises* star*
29 Bale binder
31 View from the Acropolis
32 "Just Like A Woman" singer
35 Deceptive pitch
38 Baby food may be this
40 West Florida resort
43 Of the ear
45 Bay State airport
48 Moves in a stealthy manner
50 Rockette?
52 Have ___ to play
54 Collins or Lesh
55 Brontë heroine
56 Cabinet dept.
58 Good earth
59 Aretha Franklin's sister
60 Stocking mishap
63 Triple vaccine, for short

★★ Do the Math

Enter numbers in each row and column to arrive at the end totals. Only numbers
1–9 are used and only once.

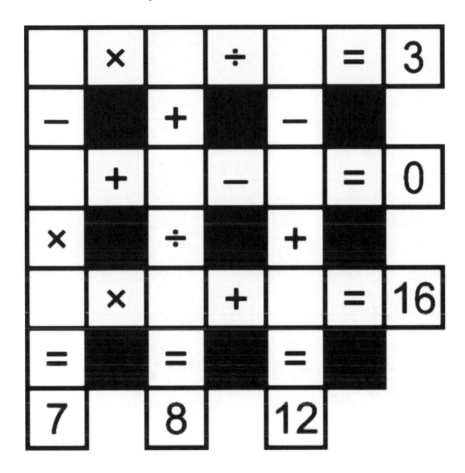

DOUBLETALK

Homophones are words that share the same pronunciation, no matter how they are spelled.
If they are spelled differently then they are called heterographs. Find heterographs meaning:

MASTICATES and SELECT

★★ BrainSnack®—Team Game

Which team (A–E) will win the competition if the logic of this diagram is continued?

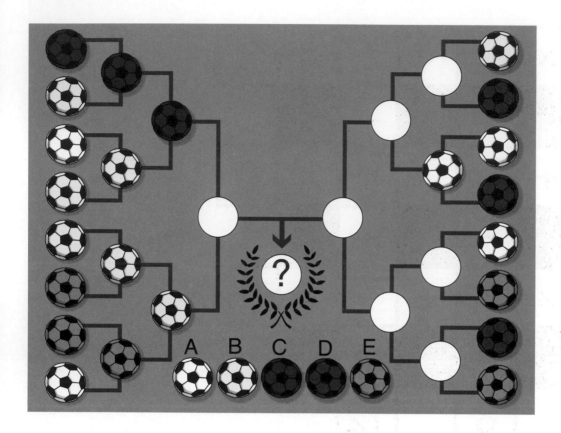

DOODLE PUZZLE

A doodle puzzle is a combination of images, letters and/or numbers that represent a word or a concept. If you cannot solve a doodle puzzle, do not look at the answer right away. Think hard—and outside the box.

★★ 2012 Movies by John M. Samson

ACROSS

1 One of the Minor Prophets
5 Overhand tennis stroke
10 32-card game
14 Avon spa
15 Second word of an apology
16 "Bond girl" Hatcher
17 2012 Tom Hanks film
19 D.C. office shape
20 Make too much of, maybe
21 Lacking imagination
23 Fossil fuel
24 "Seeing your bet ..."
25 Came out
29 Colorful, crested bird
32 Father of "gangsta" rap
33 Indeed
35 Japanese Peace Nobelist
36 Carl Maria ___ Weber
37 River of W China
38 Reader's buy, for short
39 Negev city
41 Well-padded
43 Salad shop
44 Proposer's fear
46 Pats on the back
48 Part of a long neck
49 Calorie fraction
50 Boston team
53 Human trait that fueled pirates
57 City near Moscow
58 Star of 17 Across
60 Nits, eventually
61 Page in *Juno*
62 Character hooked up with Hook
63 Requests permission
64 Camp David Accords signer
65 Proverbs

DOWN

1 "The Alphabet Song" start
2 Where Timbuktu is
3 Platte River tribe
4 No-hitter's cousin
5 Color symbol for sin
6 A purebred it's not
7 Nothing alternative
8 Ems and Baden-Baden
9 In slapdash fashion
10 Floors
11 *Here Comes the Boom* star
12 Asian shrunken sea
13 Floor covering
18 Part of DIY
22 Bird from Australia
25 David Boudia, notably
26 Where professeurs work
27 *Argo* star
28 "You know the ___!"
29 Goodyear airship
30 "I could ___ unfold...": Shak.
31 Meditation teachers
34 Inuit knife
40 Terrarium creatures
41 Certain software downloads
42 Thwart
43 Stray from a topic
45 Small whale
47 Bedouin
50 Fizzy drink
51 Sister of Ares
52 Hacienda hall
53 "___ jacta est" (the die is cast)
54 Rowling's Madam Pince
55 Henley sport
56 *Mickey Blue* ___ (1999)
59 Law degree

★ Safe Code

To open the safe you have to replace the question mark with the correct figure. You can find this figure by determining the logical method behind the numbers shown. These methods can include calculation, inversion, repetition, chronological succession, or forming ascending and descending series.

SAFE A08

CHANGELINGS

Each of the three lines of letters below spell words which have a star connection, but the letters have been mixed up. Four letters from the first word are now in the third line, four letters from the third word are in the second line and four letters from the second word are in the first line. The remaining letters are in their original places. What are the words?

S T R E R O O M A S
A S E L C N O S E R
T U P E S N O P E V

★ Word Pyramid

Each word in the pyramid has the letters of the word above it, plus a new letter.

D

(1) medical practitioner
(2) crazy
(3) Rhett's word
(4) make better
(5) evil supernatural being
(6) belly
(7) dog

DOUBLETALK

Homophones are words that share the same pronunciation, no matter how they are spelled.
If they are spelled differently then they are called heterographs. Find heterographs meaning:

RESTRAINING INFLUENCE and ROYAL AUTHORITY

★★ Sudoku

Fill in the grid so that each row, each column and each 3 x 3 frame contains every number from 1 to 9.

	9	5	1				8	
1		7	9	8		4	5	2
	8					9	6	
			8	4	2		9	
				9	5	6		4
5					7			
	6					5		
		1				2		9
7								

SYMBOL SUMS

Can you work out these number sums using three of these four symbols? **+ − ÷ ×**
(No fractions or minus numbers are involved in the sum as you progress from left to right.)

$$13 \; \square \; 10 \; \square \; 5 \; \square \; 9 = 2$$

★★★ How Sad by Mary Leonard

ACROSS

1 Midi terminus
5 Persona ___ (welcome)
10 "Super Trouper" group
14 Banned apple spray
15 In the boondocks
16 Gland ending
17 Sad writing utensil?
19 Set of threads
20 Stable gear
21 Eavesdrops
23 Not "dis"
24 Person from Pristina
25 Breakfront
29 Unhealthy
32 Leering look
33 Senior member
35 Penny in a small game
36 Herbert Hoover's wife
37 Kitten cry
38 Long in *Boyz N the Hood*
39 Cy Young winner Hershiser
41 Home run, in slang
43 Spy group
44 Dueling equipment
46 Some incentives
48 ___-tiller
49 Chess grandmaster Mikhail
50 Menacing
53 Cigars pitched by Edie Adams
57 Tarzan movie prop
58 It makes for a sad bow?
60 Subterranean soldiers
61 Colleague of Trotsky
62 Art Deco artist
63 Aberdeen girl
64 Heavenly places
65 York symbol

DOWN

1 Members of the hack pack
2 Milan's Teatro ___ Scala
3 Praise
4 Red Skelton freeloader
5 Said hello to
6 Baseball stats
7 Curved line
8 Ape's lack
9 Janney in *Juno*
10 Haydn's homeland
11 Sad hat?
12 Noah of *It Takes a Thief*
13 Newspaper section
18 Strategy
22 Gender
25 Azure, for one
26 Naxos marketplace
27 Sad snapshots?
28 Torquemada
29 More recent
30 Functional
31 Protects against tampering
34 So far
40 Elsa of *Born Free*
41 Bad news
42 Election data
43 .22, for one
45 1942 combat zone
47 Italian seaport
50 Face shape
51 Winona's *Dracula* role
52 Snowmobile
53 Chinese noodle
54 Major Spanish river
55 A boodle
56 Old blade
59 Trois less deux

★★ Futoshiki

Fill in the 5 x 5 grid with the numbers from 1 to 5 once per row and column, while following the greater than/lesser than symbols shown. There is only one valid solution that can be reached through logic and clear thinking alone!

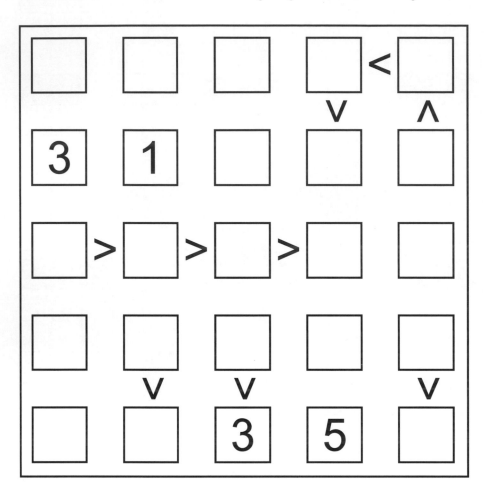

CHANGELINGS

Each of the three lines of letters below spell words or phrases relating to fine dining, but the letters have been mixed up. Four letters from the first word are now in the third line, four letters from the third word are in the second line and four letters from the second word are in the first line. The remaining letters are in their original places. What are the words?

G S S M R O L O M R
C O O M E B I E U S
A O R D T N N L E Y

★★ BrainSnack®—On Ice

With the letters in the right order, indicate the continuation of the hockey puck that starts at G–B–C–H–D–I and ends at G.

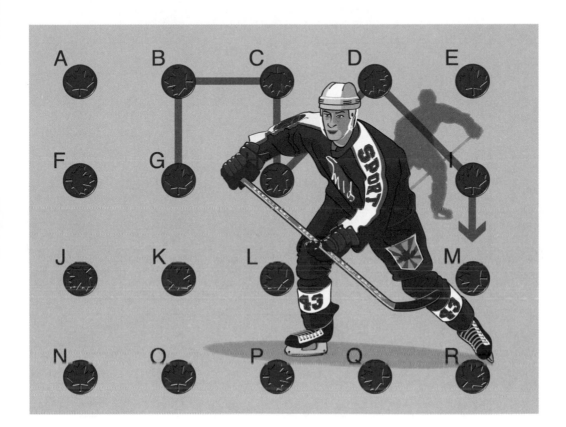

WORD WALL

Beginning at the left side of the wall, make a word by adding one group of letters from each column as you move left to right. When you have found the first word, go back to the second column and start the next word, gathering one group of letters from each column, and so on until all the letters are used to make six words.

★★★ James Bond Villains by John M. Samson

ACROSS

1 *Bill & ___ Bogus Journey* (1991)
5 Vacuums
10 Salinger dedicatee
14 Where to find most people
15 Puget Sound, e.g.
16 Bigeye fish
17 *Skyfall* villain
19 *The Court Jester* star Danny
20 Chase
21 Fireplace fixture
23 Cover girl Carol
24 Texas mesa
25 Dickered over price
29 Turns into
32 Baby powder additive
33 Fake drake
35 "Paradise" performer
36 Costa del ___
37 Hare hair
38 *Winter of Artifice* novelist
39 Rocker Rundgren
41 Ill-fated Genesis city
43 Pepper and Snorkel: Abbr.
44 Friendly
46 1972 U.S. Open champion
48 "Got it!"
49 Mad Hatter's beverage
50 Billings locale
53 Red Planet native
57 Picasso's first wife
58 First James Bond film villain
60 Look lustfully
61 Nicholas Gage heroine
62 Administers the coup de grace
63 Upper House member
64 "Crouching Woman" sculptor
65 Eyelid woe

DOWN

1 Rainy-day rollout
2 Isaac's firstborn
3 French fashion figure
4 Link in the food chain?
5 Popped in on
6 "Don't count ___"
7 "___ Follow the Sun": Beatles
8 Hindu god
9 He found Livingstone
10 Umiak rowers
11 *The Man with the Golden Gun* villain
12 Sandwich spread
13 Genesis locale
18 Sing "Rock-a-Bye Baby"
22 Savage or Severinsen
25 "___ la vista baby!"
26 Like a cold fish
27 Bond villain played by Gert Fröbe
28 *Moll Flanders* author
29 Atomic number 5
30 Pares prose
31 It can be common
34 Ruminant's chew
40 Mean coward
41 Slight
42 James Carville's better half
43 Museum marbles
45 Emmy winner Arthur
47 LPGA star ___ Pak
50 Gangster gal
51 Fake butter
52 One of the musical Guthries
53 Paul in *The Good Earth*
54 "As it ___, it ain't": Carroll
55 Raggedy Ann's brother
56 Proboscis
59 Elly May Clampett's dad

★ Picnic

All the words are hidden vertically, horizontally or diagonally—in both directions. The letters that remain unused form a sentence from left to right.

```
T T E K S A B H E I S D E F A
S N A C K S L S T W H T E R A
S S O A S B N T A I E A O E G
T O F M E S U O E N E E T N C
R R O E C N E T H E T M O C A
A E L M I L K S T S A P M H N
W P D B P I B A S E I C A B O
B P I E S M E E P A R D T R P
E E N R C S A T V P L N O E E
R P G T E O A R E E E G E A N
R I C E C I U N G K R T S D E
Y S H S S U M N D A N A I M R
J C A E R A D C T W R A G T W
A H I E N A U T O R I I L E E
M H R E L R E C I O Y C N B S
S L S A U S A G E O L A H E T
I N S E C T S S O S F E I E S
K R A P C O F F E E U N R R S
```

COOLER
COUNTRY AIR
DISH
FOLDING CHAIRS
FRENCH BREAD
GLASSES
HEAT
INSECTS
MARGARINE
MEAT
MILK
PARK
PEPPER
SALAD
SANDWICHES
SAUCES
SAUSAGE
SHEET
SNACKS
SPICES
STRAWBERRY JAM
TOMATOES
WINE

APPETITE
BASKET
BEVERAGES

BLANKET
BUTTER
CAMEMBERT

CAN OPENER
CHEESE
COFFEE

DELETE ONE

Delete one letter from NAME ALIGNED and find someone popular.

★★★ Sport Maze

Draw the shortest way from the ball to the goal. You can only move along vertical and horizontal lines, not along diagonal lines. The figure on each square indicates the number of squares the ball must be moved in the same direction. You can change direction at each stop.

4	2	5	5	2	4
1	3	3	2	2	1
1	4	0	3	0	1
4	1	1	3	4	4
1	3	3	3	3	3
0	●	2	5	3	2

ONE LETTER LESS OR MORE

The word on the right side contains the letters of the word on the left side plus or minus the letter in the middle. One letter is already in the right place.

U N D E R D O G -G ☐ ☐ U ☐ ☐ ☐ ☐

★★★ Red by John M. Samson

ACROSS

1 Woods in *Legally Blonde*
5 Young herring
10 Jug
14 Hang about
15 Arab League headquarters
16 Punching-in hour
17 RED
19 Smooth-talking
20 Honor guards, e.g.
21 Waltzer of song
23 Soak timber
24 Collette in *About a Boy*
25 Kevin in *The Bodyguard*
29 Humility
32 FDR's successor
33 Hogwash
35 *Robinson Crusoe* author
36 Ancient Hebrew lyre
38 Chalke of *Scrubs*
40 *Green Mansions* girl
41 Mature in the orchard
43 Roberts and Charles
45 Celtic sea god
46 Climb-down
48 Goddess of the hunt
50 Mull neighbor
51 Defunct space station
52 Move backward
55 Fettuccine sauce
59 Curve in the road
60 RED
62 "Dies ___" (Day of Wrath)
63 Classical east wind
64 Final Four initials
65 Auctioneer's cry
66 Brings up
67 Say it isn't true

DOWN

1 "What ___ is new?"
2 Storm systems
3 Secular
4 Earnest attempt
5 Spreads around
6 Alter egos
7 Tease
8 Jack-in-the-pulpit
9 Marinara ingredient
10 MIT athlete
11 RED
12 *The Chalk Garden* author Bagnold
13 McEntire of Nashville
18 River near Nottingham
22 Sondheim's *Sweeney ___*
25 Swiss ___
26 *Doctor Dolittle* actor Davis
27 RED
28 Beaming
29 Anne in *Awakenings*
30 Marisa in *Anger Management*
31 Biennium pair
34 ___ bono
37 Took note of
39 Non-venomous
42 Hawaiian goose
44 Far from flexible
47 Gamal of Egypt
49 Office boy's task
52 MLB Triple Crown category
53 Chair designer Aarnio
54 Elisabeth in *Hollow Man*
55 Manchurian border river
56 "Look, Lucilius!"
57 *Intensity* author Koontz
58 Scat singer Anita
61 Astral altar

★★ Letter Soup

Use up all the letters in the soup to fill in the spaces and find eight body parts.

| _ _ O _ A C H |
| _ R A I _ |
| _ R _ E _ Y |
| _ I _ G _ R |

| _ I _ N E _ |
| D _ A _ _ R A _ M |
| T _ N _ U E |
| M _ S _ _ E |

THREE-IN-ONE

Using all of the letters listed below only once, can you find the names of three major lakes of the world?

a a a b c e e i i i i k l o r r t v

★★ Sudoku X

Fill in the grid so that each row, each column and each 3 x 3 frame contains every number from 1 to 9. The two main diagonals of the grid also contain every number from 1 to 9.

						2		
8							4	1
					1	6		
9	4	2			8	5		
1			2	6		9		
	6			3	4			9
		4	9					2
3	9		1	5				8

BLOCK ANAGRAM

Form the word that is described in the brackets with the letters above the grid. Extra letters are already in the right place.

MY POOL *(market in which there is only one seller)*

		N			**O**		

★★★ 1950s Song Hits by Michele Sayer

ACROSS

1 Chrysler Building style
5 Having flavor
10 Hank Aaron's 2,297
14 "Hairy man" in Genesis 27:11
15 Accustom
16 Peter in *Dragonslayer*
17 1955 Penguins hit
19 Colorful duck
20 Some get pink slips
21 Now hear this
23 Suffix with adamant
24 Kellogg's tiger
25 Universally applicable
29 Band's number, perhaps
32 Irk
33 Opera headliners
35 *Pinky* director Kazan
36 Harmful
37 "I tawt I taw a puddy ___!"
38 Tulsa college
39 Boss Tweed's nemesis
41 Not now
43 Roulette bet
44 Level of authority
46 Orange piece
48 Jones in *Mars Attacks!*
49 Palm smartphone
50 Science of life
53 Without beginning or end
57 Profligate
58 1956 Perry Como hit
60 Chinese border river
61 Paddy in *Patriot Games*
62 Boys-only school founded in 1440
63 Boot camp lullaby
64 Rich cake
65 Florek of *Law & Order: SVU*

DOWN

1 Bottomless
2 Morales of *Caprica*
3 *Up* protagonist
4 Silhouette
5 Irish moss, e.g.
6 Curry and Coulter
7 Curly-tailed dog
8 Raised the hackles of
9 Does away with, electronically
10 Entourage
11 1957 Everly Brothers hit
12 Requiem hymn word
13 Move cars
18 Respond to a bumper sticker
22 Chicken, to a French chef
25 Pickle juice
26 Sachet scent
27 1957 Elvis Presley hit
28 Cronus, e.g.
29 Uses a scale from 1 to 10
30 Noise associated with police
31 Razz
34 Brewery tank
40 S&L employees
41 The ___ Summer (1958)
42 Dinosaur, e.g.
43 Came to light
45 Film doctor with seven faces
47 Diver Louganis
50 Dennis the Menace, e.g.
51 "___ Rock": Simon & Garfunkel
52 Former city near Tokyo
53 Doctor documents
54 Silent actress Naldi
55 "This must weigh ___!"
56 Redgrave in *Shine*
59 Cousin of tri-

★★ BrainSnack®—Pop Numbers

Which number should replace the question mark?

QUICK CROSSWORD

Place the book-related words listed below in the crossword grid.

BLOCK COPY DENTS DEVICE FAKE FOLIO HEAD ISSUE LOOSE SHEET SIZE STUB

★★ Do the Math

Enter numbers in each row and column to arrive at the end totals. Only numbers 1–9 are used and only once.

	−		×		=	1
÷		+		×		
	+		÷		=	2
×		−		+		
	−		+		=	10
=		=		=		
6		11		14		

TRIANAGRAM

Three-word groups of anagrams are called triplets or trianagrams.
Complete the group:

TRUCE _ _ _ _ _   _ _ _ _ _

★★★ 1960s Song Hits by Michele Sayer

ACROSS

1 Nobel Peace Center city
5 Expire, as a subscription
10 Black-and-white duck
14 Drawing card
15 Jong who wrote *Fanny*
16 Popular belief
17 1969 Archies hit
19 First-class
20 Desist from
21 Mixed
23 Prefix meaning "egg"
24 Nickname of Dr. Henry Jones
25 Teenage TV witch
29 Have coming
32 ___ *Well That Ends Well*
33 Fingerpaint
35 Cambodian currency
36 Inuit knife
37 Wood-smoothing tool
38 Itinerary word
39 Virginia whitetail
41 Potok's Lev
43 Bloke
44 Contrives
46 Manifold
48 Tel Aviv carrier
49 Suffix for ball
50 Gary of *Diff'rent Strokes*
53 Maid of ___ (Joan of Arc)
57 Thomas ___ Edison
58 1962 Shirelles hit
60 Roger of *Double Platinum*
61 Al Capone nemesis Ness
62 *East of Eden* brother
63 Behind schedule
64 Nazareth native, e.g.
65 Queue

DOWN

1 Olympus Mountains peak
2 Show souvenir
3 Falls behind
4 Figures of speech?
5 Wounds
6 Make ___ for it (flee)
7 Pen pal?
8 Evidence of injury
9 Closer to the start
10 Speak ill of
11 1961 Pat Boone hit
12 Sea swooper
13 Garden woe
18 Shankar of sitar fame
22 Type spacers
25 King Abdullah subject
26 *I've Got a Secret* host Steve
27 1963 Bobby Vinton hit
28 Get together
29 ___ and confused
30 Coal concentrations
31 Make giddy
34 Letter in runes
40 Sublet free
41 Country albums?
42 Abbott and Costello film
43 Star soldier?
45 Skater Naomi Nari ___
47 Lemming cousin
50 Poet Sandburg
51 Olive genus
52 *Show Boat* heroine
53 Bad smell
54 Shelter dug into a hillside
55 AM-PM connection
56 "... for auld lang ___"
59 Canadian pol. party

★★ Kakuro

Each number in a black area is the sum of the numbers that you have to enter in the next empty boxes. The empty boxes that make up the sum are called a run. The sum of the across run is written above the diagonal in the black area and the sum of the down run is written below the diagonal. Runs can only contain the numbers 1 through 9 and each number in a run can only be used once. The gray boxes only contain odd numbers and the white only even numbers.

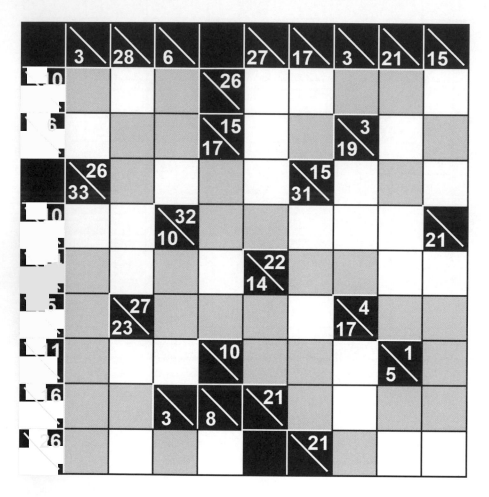

DOUBLETALK

Homophones are words that share the same pronunciation, no matter how they are spelled. If they are spelled differently then they are called heterographs. Find heterographs meaning:

GIVE OFF A STRONG SMELL and TO INFLICT OR CAUSE

★★ Sudoku Twin

Fill in the grid so that each row, each column and each 3 x 3 frame contains every number from 1 to 9. A sudoku twin is two connected 9 x 9 sudokus.

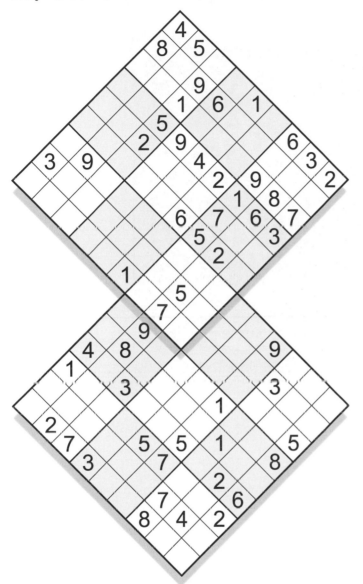

TRIANAGRAM

Three-word groups of anagrams are called triplets or trianagrams.
Complete the group:

P O R E D _ _ _ _ _ _ _ _ _ _

★★ BrainSnack®—A Bad Year?

Which year does not belong?

CLOCKWISE

The answers to the clues from 1 to 12 are all seven-letter words which
end with the letter Y. When you have solved the puzzle correctly,
working clockwise from 1, the twelve letters in the outer circle
will spell the name of a hobby popular with outdoors types.

1 Budapest's country
2 Iliad's sequel
3 Unkempt
4 Comedy opposite
5 Figurative language
6 Group of actors
7 Montevideo's land
8 Allegiance
9 Concisely, curtly
10 Extraordinary
11 Likely to break
12 Thrift

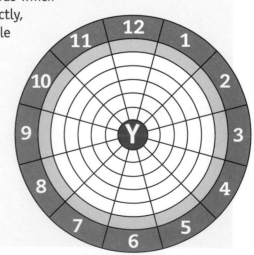

★ 1970s Song Hits by Michele Sayer

ACROSS

1 Train for a fight
5 Play charades
10 Large
14 White House employee
15 Mister, in Mexico
16 Stratford river
17 1970 Carpenters hit
19 Hit the books
20 Takes a rest
21 Concert souvenirs
23 Sharp
24 Sharp taste
25 Finger, so to speak
27 FBI leader
30 Lustful
33 Parboil
35 "Somebody" singer McEntire
36 "Exodus" hero
37 SEC team
38 Long time
39 Woes
41 Basho composition
43 Closefitting
44 1988 Schwarzenegger film
46 Dortmund duck
48 Frayed
49 Knocked off
53 Salad fruit
56 Citrus fruit
57 Seaport of Eire
58 1971 Rolling Stones hit
60 Fanning in *We Bought a Zoo*
61 ___ Bell (Anne Brontë)
62 Guitar ancestor
63 Fred in *Sanford and Son*
64 Boastful
65 Dregs

DOWN

1 Pelvis bones
2 Coin stacks, e.g.
3 Take under one's wing
4 Ring out
5 Holds highly
6 Avant-gardists
7 At all
8 Gaffer
9 Depended on
10 Spacecraft sent to Mercury
11 1976 Barbra Streisand hit
12 Zodiac animal
13 Added details
18 "¿Como ___ usted?"
22 Dined on
26 Grandiose display
27 Lucky shot
28 Hassan of *Arabian Nights*
29 Lana of Smallville
30 Hideaway
31 Oilman Halliburton
32 1970 Cat Stevens hit
34 ___ *Am* (Alicia Keys album)
40 Taken back
41 Clutch purse
42 Beyond the ordinary
43 Beach bird
45 Paleozoic, for one
47 Olympian ideals
50 Smooth shift
51 Thrill
52 Vandy team
53 Pacer in *Cars 2*
54 Rodent with a short tail
55 Killer whale
56 Ark groupings
59 NFL tiebreakers

★ Poetry

All the words are hidden vertically, horizontally or diagonally—in both directions. The letters that remain unused form a sentence from left to right.

```
O A R E P O E M T I D Y L L V
D D O N S E X T E T A G O I E
E S M S O N N E T N Z E L M A
O Y A S M M E T C H N L A E L
H V N A E A T S O O A E F R P
O L C T L R D O N N T V W I O
V A E I F G I R E O S I X C C
O N C R E I E L I D N S M K E
C D O E P P L T E G R U B E A
A A U I I E S O R P A A U C N
L L P E T E R C N O C L R L D
I L L D A A L E F I N P L O I
Z A E T P E T D L Y D O E G L
E B T O H E S N D N O E S U A
D I S T I C H T E I H T Q E N
D I T H Y R A M B M R R U A O
P A S T O R A L V E A Y E T T
O R H Y M E C A N T I L E N A
```

ECLOGUE
ELEGY
EPIGRAM
EPITAPH
HYMN
IDYLL
LAMENTATION
LIMERICK
MADRIGAL
NONSENSE
OCTET
ODE
PASTORAL
PROSE
RIDDLE
ROMANCE
SATIRE
SEXTET
SONNET
STANZA
VILLANELLE
VISUAL POETRY
VOCALIZE

ATONAL
BALLAD
BURLESQUE
CANTILENA
CONCRETE
COPLA
COUPLET
DISTICH
DITHYRAMB

DELETE ONE

Delete one letter from JIVE PATTERN and find a trapping of great wealth.

★ Hourglass

Starting in the middle, each word in the top half has the letters of the word below it, plus a new letter, and each word in the bottom half has the letters of the word above it, plus a new letter.

(1) rock group
(2) barn
(3) sound of sheep or goats
(4) capable

(5) round object
(6) mark
(7) legally responsible
(8) free

UNCANNY TURN

Rearrange the letters of the phrase below to form a cognate anagram, one which is related or connected in meaning to the original phrase. The answer can be one or more words.

A DOMESTICATED ANIMAL

★★★ 1980s Song Hits by Michele Sayer

ACROSS

1 Lone Ranger's wear
5 All washed up?
10 Hence
14 Toledo's lake
15 German soprano Lehmann
16 Unpleasant destiny
17 1980 Dolly Parton hit
19 Minutes
20 Can't stand
21 Kodiak Islander
23 Scots uncle
24 Prefix meaning "Chinese"
25 Make one's mark
29 Fundraiser
32 Audible dashes
33 Shakespeare's Athenian hermit
35 Steakhouse request
36 Spanish bear
37 "Crying" singer Orbison
38 Book before Exod.
39 Oceans
41 Gave in
43 Romantically wowed
44 Poked around
46 Lays down
48 Put on weight
49 Summa ___ laude
50 Bring under control
53 It may be poetic
57 "Yipes!"
58 1980 Diana Ross hit
60 Tears in two
61 Witherspoon in *Sweet Home Alabama*
62 *Diary of ___ Housewife* (1970)
63 Part of London's West End
64 Emends
65 Hankerings

DOWN

1 Convalesce
2 Racing's Luyendyk
3 Seven are deadly
4 They're worth holding on to
5 Least distant
6 Severe sentence
7 Judge served by Samuel
8 Inventive middle name?
9 Leslie who played Magoo
10 *Roots* Emmy winner
11 1983 Def Leppard hit
12 "I ___ Name": Croce
13 Neighbor of Yemen
18 "Long ___ Gone": Dixie Chicks
22 Rhone tributary
25 Images of gods
26 Chimney builder
27 1983 Def Leppard hit
28 Parented
29 Charles in *Gaslight*
30 Tango popularizer Castle
31 Revival places
34 Avant-garde
40 Scoundrel
41 Don't just chide
42 Determines
43 Hoped-for time
45 "Honey ___": Beatles
47 Purple shade
50 That girl's
51 Money changer's commission
52 Put the pedal to the metal
53 Tilt, asea
54 Iditarod Trail end
55 Ballet lake
56 Quits
59 Sardine whale

★★ Maze—Alternate Colors

Enter and exit the maze where indicated. You may pass over a colored square, but you must alternate between passing red and green squares or vice versa.

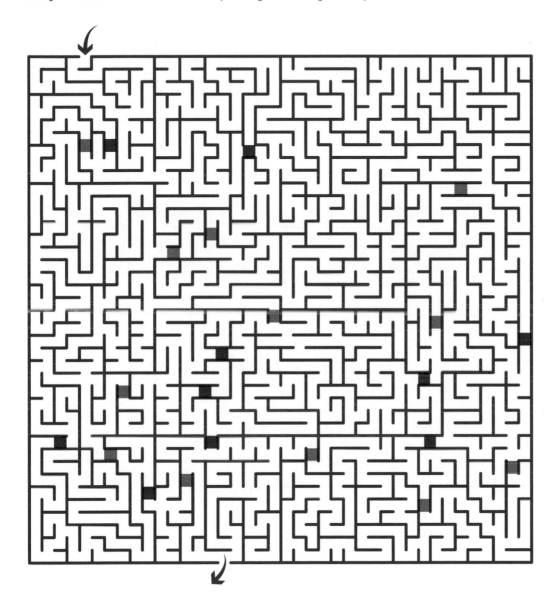

FRIENDS?

What do the following words have in common?

BOREDOM FLUMMOX RAMPAGE TOUSLED MESSINESS SPECTACULARLY

★★ Word Parts

Place the left and right word parts with the middle letters to form six new words.

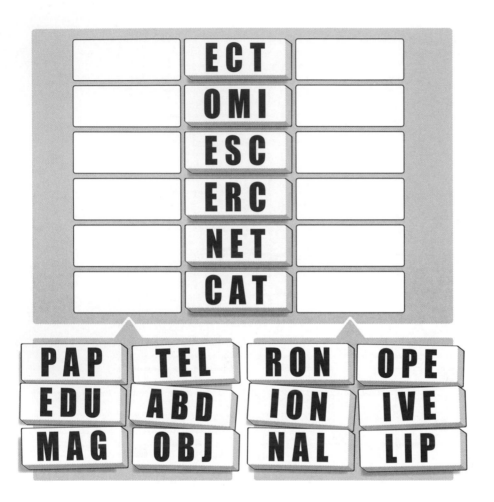

ONE LETTER LESS OR MORE

The word on the right side contains the letters of the word on the left side plus or minus the letter in the middle. One letter is already in the right place.

L O C A T I N G +S ☐ ☐ S ☐ ☐ ☐ ☐ ☐ ☐

★★★ Familiarity by Mary Leonard

ACROSS

1 Battles royal
5 Turkish pooh-bah
10 Broadcast
14 Stonestreet of *Modern Family*
15 Miscalculated
16 Survey responses, e.g.
17 *The Sting* star?
19 Texas college
20 Moreover
21 Amelia Earhart's plane
23 ___ *for Burglar*: Grafton
24 Jack in *Rio Lobo*
25 Doesn't go along
29 Text fixers
32 2012 Olympics VIP
33 Falcon nail
35 Common car
36 Skye caps
38 Evans or Blair
40 Impromptu screwdriver
41 Irish patriot (1778-1803)
43 Comes down hard
45 *Fresh Air* airer
46 McCormick's machines
48 Ask
50 Check entry
51 Wine barrel
52 Superlative for Snow White
55 Whet
59 Noted Kenyan lioness
60 *Look Homeward, Angel* author?
62 Hot stuff
63 Cat Nation members
64 "Sure, why don't we?"
65 "Clair de ___": Debussy
66 Famed thesaurian
67 Hindmost

DOWN

1 Jack who played Friday
2 Arafura Sea islands
3 Barbecue favorites
4 Writer
5 Stand in the Louvre
6 Kennel sounds
7 Sellout indicator
8 Word said while raising a hand
9 Perplexed
10 Like some guesses
11 *Full Metal Jacket* star?
12 Way for Cato
13 Spanish appetizer
18 Dictum
22 First Olympic site
25 Lash LaRue film, e.g.
26 Hold responsible
27 Jefferson's successor?
28 Makes the cut
29 Bitter-___ (die-hard)
30 Level connections
31 Hägar the Horrible's pet
34 Ketel ___ vodka
37 Break up
39 February birthstone
42 Beret holder
44 ___ Valley, CA
47 Breather
49 Ready the red carpet
52 Took a nosedive
53 Dominican baseball family
54 Matador's adversary
55 *Finding Neverland* role
56 It may be entered in a court
57 Salamanders
58 Bird's-___ soup
61 Russian jet

★★ BrainSnack®—Red Blooded

There is something wrong with which red blood cell (1–5)?

LETTER LINE

Put a letter in each of the squares below to make a word that describes "suggested instructions." The number clues refer to other words that can be made from the whole.

6 5 1 9 8 4 HANDED-DOWN STORY; 10 6 5 4 1 9
SNOW VEHICLE; 4 5 3 1 8 TO THINK WORTHY OF ONESELF;
8 2 4 1 9 PUSH GENTLY; 1 2 3 6 5 CRAFTY BEHAVIOR

1	2	3	4	5	6	7	8	9	10

★★ Word Sudoku

Complete the grid so that each row, each column and each 3 x 3 frame contains the nine letters from the black box below. The hidden nine-letter word is in the diagonal from top left to bottom right.

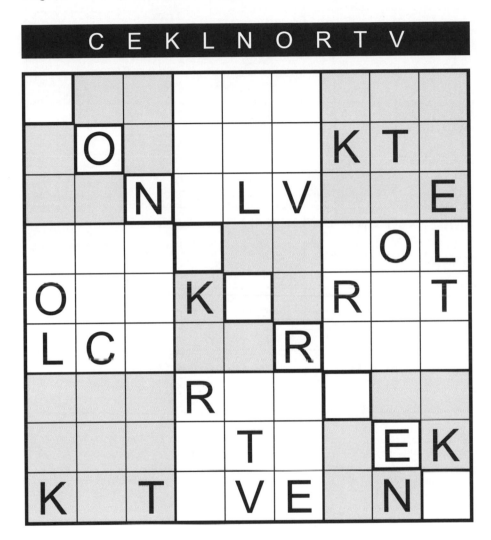

C E K L N O R T V

THREE-IN-ONE

Using all of the letters listed below only once, can you find the surnames of three classic American writers?

a a e g h h h i i n n n o o r r r t t v w w

★★★ This and That by Maggie Ellis

ACROSS

1 Chipping targets
5 Buoyant wood
10 Prepare potatoes
14 Colorful tropical fish
15 24-book epic poem
16 Wrinkly fruit
17 Planting season
19 Nabors portrayal
20 Like a junior miss
21 Lost one's footing
23 Get there or get here
24 Cool sounding rapper?
25 Costner role in a 1987 film
27 Whenever
30 Urban brume
33 Brief and to the point
35 Sidle of *CSI*
36 Spinning toy
37 Ember coating
38 ___ *for Noose*: Grafton
39 Response to an error
41 John who was knighted
43 "Over here ..."
44 Methodology
46 Rock's Jethro ___
48 Elective at VPI
49 Ends
53 Tire given a new lease on life
56 Like king crab
57 Quilter's accessory case
58 Rate per hundred
60 *Death in Venice* author
61 Comforter of Job
62 Intestinal divisions
63 Puckster Petrov
64 A hexagon has six
65 King or queen

DOWN

1 ___ del Sol
2 Bunk option
3 Kitchen knife
4 Fulgent
5 Superlative for the blue whale
6 German oldster
7 Half of CIV
8 Peckinpah and Perkins
9 "Flower of my heart" in song
10 Punch and Judy
11 Giza natives
12 *Mademoiselle* rival
13 Failed the polygraph
18 Central church area
22 Cool
26 Naval commandos
27 Take ___ at (attempt)
28 Radiology pictures
29 Brooklyn Bridge river
30 "Quit it!"
31 Opponent of El Cid
32 Auspicious
34 They come before U
40 Getting the point
41 Houdini feats
42 Chromosome home
43 Paper alternative
45 Antibes summer
47 Spindly
50 Oscar nominee Lilia
51 Rarin' to go
52 Three-time Masters winner
53 Riviera's San ___
54 Collective abbr.
55 It has a meaty role
56 Feel pity
59 Cleansed

★★★ Sudoku

Fill in the grid so that each row, each column and each 3 x 3 frame contains every number from 1 to 9.

					1	5		8
			3	5	6		7	4
		5						
8		7	9					
				7	8	2	5	1
		3	6		4			
		8	5	1	2	3		6
4	6				7			

SYMBOL SUMS

Can you work out these number sums using three of these four symbols? **+ − ÷ ×**
(No fractions or minus numbers are involved in the sum as you progress from left to right.)

$$52 \; \square \; 4 \; \square \; 6 \; \square \; 5 = 40$$

★ Word Ladders

Convert the word at the top of the ladders into the word at the bottom, using all the rungs in between. On each rung, you must put a valid word that has the same letters as the word above it, apart from one letter change. There may be more than one way of achieving this.

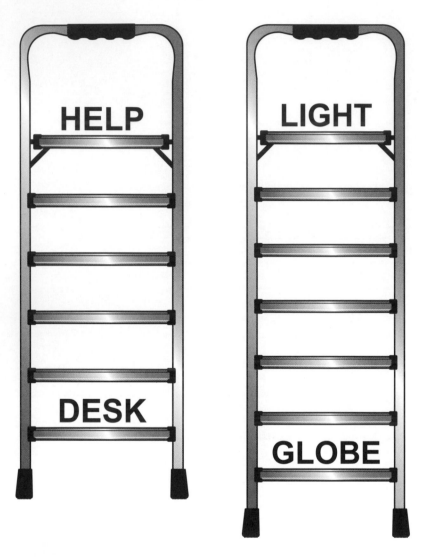

SANDWICH

What five-letter word belongs between the word on the left and the word on the right, so that the first and second word, and the second and third word, each form a common compound word or phrase?

HEAD _ _ _ _ _ LINE

★★★ Eclectic Mix by Maggie Ellis

ACROSS

1 Dressed
5 Censor out
10 Early George Michael duo
14 Audition topic
15 Depart
16 Castlebar locale
17 Lord or lady
19 Pierce the perforation
20 Inferior to
21 Patches up
23 *Hägar the Horrible* dog
24 Creek at Augusta National
25 Pavilion
28 It lays the largest egg
31 Org. that fights price-fixing
34 Jackson & Perkins hybrids
36 Clothe
37 Chain with edible links
39 Chef Batali
41 Arista
42 Biblical whale bait
44 Bass Pro Shop line
46 Wane
47 Entrance
49 Pull apart
51 *La Belle ___ Bête*: Philip Glass
52 Mighty peculiar
56 Charles in *The Sting*
59 Used frying pans
61 "Of course!"
62 Coach dogs
64 Swerve
65 ___-propre (self-esteem)
66 Punta del ___
67 Trattoria seafood
68 Rock shelf
69 "Kiss From a Rose" singer

DOWN

1 Fiddlers and hermits
2 Sophia in *The Millionairess*
3 Roomy dress cut
4 Rommel's milieu
5 Imperfection
6 Poland's Walesa
7 Musician's need
8 Perón and Marie Saint
9 Bernadette in *The Jerk*
10 Horse operas
11 What kids might roll down
12 "I Am Not My Hair" singer India.___
13 New York nine
18 Spud
22 *The Help* director Taylor
26 Nice name?
27 Romanov rulers
28 Wicker willow
29 Precious
30 LeBron James's team
31 Vijay Singh's homeland
32 Suffix with tele
33 Snaky fish
35 Poet's preposition
38 Mates
40 Fronton encouragement
43 Prefix for copter
45 Rhino feature
48 Key West shoe
50 Import taxes
53 Do a salon job
54 Alamo ___ Car
55 Ford of 1957
56 Dumpy bar
57 Plaintiff
58 Undaunted
59 Self-satisfied
60 Swiss border river
63 Ben Gurion Airport locale

★★ Futoshiki

Fill in the 5 x 5 grid with the numbers from 1 to 5 once per row and column, while following the greater than/lesser than symbols shown. There is only one valid solution that can be reached through logic and clear thinking alone!

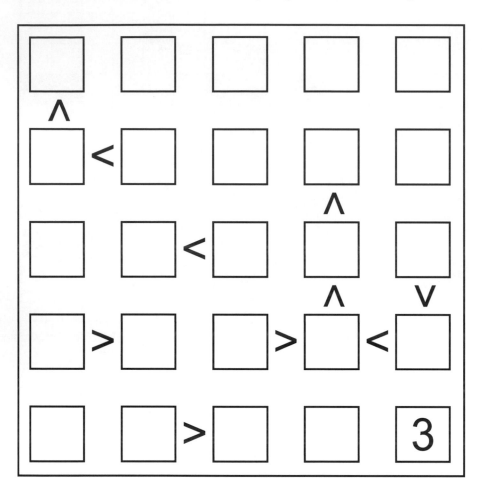

LETTERBLOCKS

Move the letterblocks around so that words are formed on top and below that you can associate with the circus. In some blocks, the letter from the top row has been switched with the letter from the bottom row.

B	A	A	E	O	R	C
E	T	Z	T	P	A	R

★★ BrainSnack®—Angles

You see the same cube from three different angles. You can complete the cube with the six pieces. Which piece (1–6) is not useful?

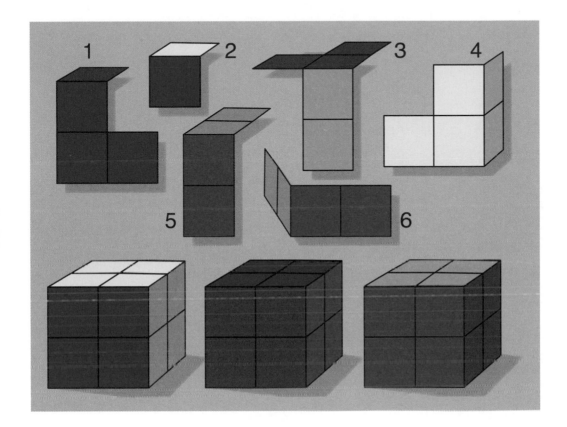

DOODLE PUZZLE

A doodle puzzle is a combination of images, letters and/or numbers that represent a word or a concept. If you cannot solve a doodle puzzle, do not look at the answer right away. Think hard—and outside the box.

★ Carnivorans

All the words are hidden vertically, horizontally or diagonally—in both directions. The letters that remain unused form a sentence from left to right.

```
N X O F C E N N E F O T A L X
L C A R N I B I N T U R O N G
G O L D E N C A T V O R Y A A
R T A C D E L B R A M L N M T
E D R A P O E L W O N S S U A
G A R J U N G L E C A T C P K
D N R A E B H T O L S H A E R
A O C A R R N I V O E A R R E
B I G R E S M T H E R T A E E
Y L M N P A N I D A V E C G M
E R A A I I S C N A A E A I V
N A R J N D E L O E L H L T E
O C T A G E A T E A T C A R H
H O E C I E D A O N T T H Y A
T O N K S P F W R Y I I E M A
R N J A G U A R O I O N S L Y
E W A L R U S A E L A C T S B
E S O O G N O M A T F M B O O
```

GOLDEN CAT
HONEY BADGER
HYENA
JACKAL
JAGUAR
JUNGLE CAT
LION
LYNX
MANED WOLF
MARBLED CAT
MARTEN
MEERKAT
MONGOOSE
PUMA
RACOON
SEAL
SERVAL
SLOTH BEAR
SNOW LEOPARD
TIGER
WALRUS

BINTURONG
CARACAL
CHEETAH

COATIS
COYOTE
DINGO

ERMINE
FENNEC FOX
FRET

DELETE ONE

Delete one letter from ATTACH LONG SORRY and find something you may consult to see ahead.

★★★★ Paradise by John M. Samson

ACROSS

1 Dapper Dan's concern
5 Stared in wonder
10 Bluish color
14 On the Atlantic
15 Love, Italian-style
16 Balanced
17 "Leader of the Pack" group
19 Sunrise location, in Spain
20 Individuals
21 Run roughly, as an engine
23 Color
24 "Not ___ many words ..."
25 Marathoner Salazar
29 "Falling in Love" singer Gloria
32 Got fired up
33 Hulu offering
35 Robot in *WALL-E*
36 The world, to Atlas
37 Swift
38 "Zip-___-Doo-Dah"
39 "You Won't ___ Me": Beatles
40 American canonized in 1975
41 Edgar Bergen dummy
42 Make more appealing
44 Résumé parts
46 "Popular Fallacies" essayist
47 Resin used in varnish
48 Yammer
51 Asks "What if?"
55 Contain
56 New Brunswick vacation spot
58 Petits-fours finisher
59 Media attraction
60 Harnessed Clydesdales
61 Telephoto or contact
62 Hailstorm damage
63 Slippery varmints

DOWN

1 ("I'm shocked!")
2 NYC's Arthur ___ Stadium
3 Hindmost
4 Wailing spirits
5 Dark red gem
6 *Jake's Thing* author
7 D.C. dignitary
8 Stats at Cooperstown
9 Felt enmity toward
10 Congo fly
11 James Dean film
12 Texas Hold'em stake
13 Give the eye to
18 Calabash
22 Golden Rule word
25 Sprang up
26 Sheets and such
27 Steve Martin film (with *My*)
28 Like pear tree leaves
29 *Absolutely Fabulous* role
30 Adroitly avoid
31 Requires
34 NASDAQ newbie
37 Remembered
38 Cosby specialty
40 Bad state
41 Exiguous
43 Lets down, in a sense
45 Hits hard
48 Famous groundhog
49 Three-legged ___
50 Christmas lights site
51 Shoved off
52 Electric sword
53 Yemeni dough
54 Walmart club
57 Watanabe in *The Last Samurai*

★ Spot the Differences

Find the nine differences in the image on the right.

DOUBLETALK

Homophones are words that share the same pronunciation, no matter how they are spelled. If they are spelled differently then they are called heterographs. Find heterographs meaning:

COMPLETE and A DEMAND FOR PAYMENT

★ Word Wheel

How many words of three or more letters, each including the letter at the center of the wheel, can you make from this diagram? No plurals or conjugations. We've found 13, including one nine-letter word. Can you do better?

DOODLE PUZZLE

A doodle puzzle is a combination of images, letters and/or numbers that represent a word or a concept. If you cannot solve a doodle puzzle, do not look at the answer right away. Think hard—and outside the box.

★★★★ Themeless by Don Law

ACROSS
1 Spice Girls hit
5 Saudi coin
10 *Jolly Roger* crewman
14 Others, to Cicero
15 Barclays Center, for one
16 Mountain lake
17 Funny business
19 Idaho motto word
20 Draw a cartoon
21 Pokes holes in a lawn
23 Like some twangs
24 Midway attraction
25 *La Strada* composer Rota
28 Person with goals
31 Scottish coastal resort
34 Grain alcohol component
36 Borden cow
37 *The Sunshine ___* (1975)
39 Actress Veronica
41 Days gone by
42 Colorful mineral
44 Carnival peep show
46 Nemo's harpoonist
47 Founder of Reprise Records
49 Turns out doilies
51 Not fooled by
52 Inventor of root beer
56 Biker headwear
59 Nobelist France from France
61 Region
62 2012 Daniel Day-Lewis role
64 Imminent
65 Amy Lowell's flower
66 Small bills
67 Klondike discovery of 1897
68 Colonial diplomat Silas
69 Scant

DOWN
1 Hunter of the PGA
2 Honey Boo Boo
3 Small wheels
4 QB-turned-sportscaster Troy
5 Fully absorbed
6 "Dies ___" (funeral hymn)
7 Japanese coin
8 "Lonely Boy" singer Paul
9 Lasagna features
10 With regularity
11 Mary Stuart in *Benny and Joon*
12 Art Deco name
13 Book of Mormon book
18 Rival of a Princetonian
22 Like a black blackberry
26 Advanced degree?
27 Maureen of *The Quiet Man*
28 Standing at the ready
29 Waterford locale
30 Fipple flute, for one
31 Garments made of camel's hair
32 Hall-of-Famer Berra
33 *Paper Moon* actor
35 Peru's Sumac
38 "Spring ahead" time
40 Shepherd's place
43 "Miss Peaches" James
45 Frome of literature
48 McDonald's clown
50 *The Office* is one
53 *Nightline* creator Arledge
54 Aunt Murphy in *Oklahoma!*
55 Have an inkling
56 Pistol pop
57 Mars: Comb. form
58 Gymnastics coach Grossfeld
59 Astronaut Shepard
60 Riviera resort
63 Heart test

★★ BrainSnack®—Snow Fun

Which snow flake (1–10) does not belong?

WORD WALL

Beginning at the left side of the wall, make a
word by adding one group of letters from each
column as you move left to right. When you
have found the first word, go back to the second
column and start the next word, gathering one
group of letters from each column, and so on
until all the letters are used to make six words.

★★ The Puzzled Librarian

The new library assistant accidentally bumped into the Good Reads notice board, and the magnetic letters all fell off. The librarian remembered the authors' names, but needs some help to get the titles right, as the chief librarian will be back in ten minutes!

GOOD READS NOTICE BOARD

1. SEMI NEW by Stuart Nadler
2. END HINTER by Herman Koch
3. A STRIFE STRIVING FIEND by Michael Hainey
4. ICED LOGO by Amity Shlaes
5. SANITY NICE by Dave Barry
6. CAPABLE HUNTER by Stephen Dobyns
7. I ROTTED by Charlie LeDuff
8. MATH SONG by Roger Hobbs
9. A BESEECHING TENTH OWLET by M.L. Stedman
10. FICTIVE ILLUSORY by Amor Towles

DOODLE PUZZLE

A doodle puzzle is a combination of images, letters and/or numbers that represent a word or a concept. If you cannot solve a doodle puzzle, do not look at the answer right away. Think hard—and outside the box.

★★★★ Themeless by Don Law

ACROSS
1 Owls of the NCAA
5 Whitman's bloomer
10 Young elephant
14 Arabian Sea gulf
15 *Cosmicomics* author Calvino
16 Slangy ending for buck
17 *Horrible Bosses* actress
20 Go-ahead
21 Blameless
22 Palm Springs, for one
24 Ward with an Emmy
25 Free from liability
28 Railroad employee
32 "I took the one ___ traveled by": Frost
33 Trudeau or Kasparov
35 Chair designer Aarnio
36 Blonde shade
37 ___ kwon do
38 *Le Monde* article
39 Drudgery
41 Football foursome
43 Force
44 Go up against
46 SAT takers
48 Some edible roots
50 In a state of amazement
51 Step up
55 Does a teacher's job
58 *Destry Rides Again* star
60 "___ You Babe": Sonny & Cher
61 "Rehearsal of a Ballet" painter
62 "Rosanna" rock group
63 Like Victorian collars
64 Exhausted
65 Top of Old Smokey

DOWN
1 Rangoon royal
2 Caesar's last day
3 Press suppression
4 Groups of nine
5 Bodybuilder's practice
6 Suffix for New Jersey
7 "Now I Know" singer White
8 Cranston and Dershowitz
9 *Diamonds Are Forever* star
10 Torrent
11 *Laugh-In* regular Johnson
12 "Laughing" bird
13 Garamond, e.g.
18 Kid Rock's "___ Deep"
19 Captive of Hercules
23 Defense pact of 1954–77
25 Student of Socrates
26 "The Wolf in Sheep's Clothing" writer
27 Some chess endings
29 "My Heart Will Go On" singer
30 "___ We All?"
31 Foreign assignments
34 Designer Oscar de la ___
40 Allegiance
41 Ultimatums
42 Get at
43 Exits
45 Circular announcement
47 Scurry
49 Make thoroughly wet
51 Jannings of filmdom
52 Epic narrative
53 River dragon
54 Outskirts
56 Prefix meaning "outer"
57 Exhibit
59 *Atonement* author McEwan

★ Hourglass

Starting in the middle, each word in the top half has the letters of the word below it, plus a new letter, and each word in the bottom half has the letters of the word above it, plus a new letter.

(1) cry out
(2) spitefulness
(3) mammal
(4) not agitated

(5) bivouac
(6) muscular contraction
(7) motor home
(8) equate

SYMBOL SUMS

Can you work out these number sums using three of these four symbols? **+ − ÷ ×**
(No fractions or minus numbers are involved in the sum as you progress from left to right.)

$$38 \; \square \; 2 \; \square \; 18 \; \square \; 4 = 33$$

★★ Maze—Binoculars

Enter the maze, pass over all binoculars from behind (thereby disabling them) and then exit. You may not pass through a grid space more than once, and may not enter a grid space in the line of binoculars you have not yet disabled.

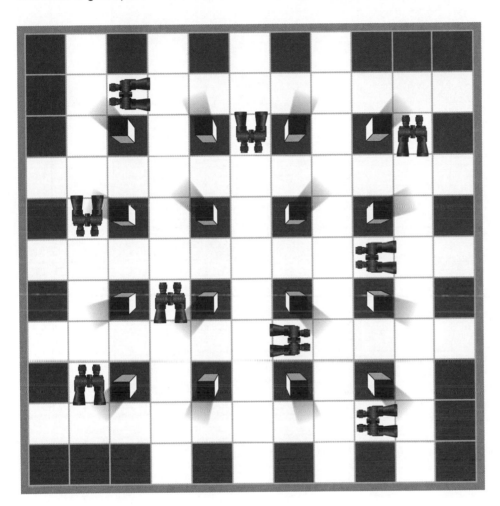

FRIENDS?

What do the following words have in common?

HE MAT TEND ELECT SQUAD MAGNET WAIT DIGIT

★★★★ Olio by Cindy Nell

ACROSS

1 *The Morning Watch* novelist
5 Pallet filling
10 Colossal, for olives
14 Like shad
15 Cook by simmering
16 In a bit, to the bard
17 Hazy
19 Sparks, Nevada neighbor
20 Motioned to
21 Splits to unite
23 Loki's troublemaker
24 *Treasure Island* captain
25 Finney in *Big Fish*
28 Desperately hanging on
31 Kind of role actors like
32 Guthrie's "___ for Glory"
33 Shop ___ you drop
34 1970 Donald Sutherland film
35 Goliath killer
36 Olympic sled
37 Set a price for
38 Monkeying around?
39 Lies low
40 Inessential
42 Some are designer
43 Hawthorne's were "twice-told"
44 Chess notation
45 ___ domain
47 Nutritionist's concerns
51 Cameo shape
52 Carolina NHL team
54 Ward in *Double Jeopardy*
55 Toss out
56 Civil offense
57 "Malle Babbe" painter
58 "Fierce" alter ego of Beyoncé
59 Aphrodite's love child

DOWN

1 "... and carry ___ stick": Roosevelt
2 Departed
3 Draws to a close
4 Canines that bite
5 Essence
6 Color wheel display
7 Worry for a speakeasy patron
8 Don't just sit there
9 West Virginia's "Friendly City"
10 Malaysian skirt
11 Incompetence
12 District
13 Book of Mormon book
18 Like Chewbacca
22 "Swedish Nightingale" Jenny
24 Tossed
25 King Abdullah's city
26 Landlord's contract
27 Sport with a shot clock
28 Numismatist's loves
29 Bruce of Dr. Watson fame
30 *Cagney & Lacey* star
32 Ignorance, at times
35 Soliloquies
36 Emancipate
38 "That's ___ need!"
39 Wrack
41 Victoria Principal series
42 Sue Lyon title role
44 "Madness" month
45 Luxurious
46 Eye membrane
47 Sportscaster Collinsworth
48 "Are you ___ out?"
49 Bubble Chair designer Aarnio
50 Former boomers
53 Cavaliers of the ACC

★★★ Sport Maze

Draw the shortest way from the ball to the goal. You can only move along
vertical and horizontal lines, not along diagonal lines. The figure on each square
indicates the number of squares the ball must be moved in the same direction.
You can change direction at each stop.

1	3	4	1	3	2
2	4	3	○	2	5
3	4	3	3	2	4
2	2	2	1	2	4
5	1	4	0	3	1
4	3	1	1	4	5

CHANGELINGS

Each of the three lines of letters below spell words which are courses you might study at
college, but the letters have been mixed up. Four letters from the first word are now in the third
line, four letters from the third word are in the second line and four letters from the second
word are in the first line. The remaining letters are in their original places. What are the words?

H I O E R P T U Y E
P U I L N S O I H M
J O L R T A L A S R

★★ BrainSnack®—No Graffiti

Each spray can has three symbols indicating how many harmful propellants are in that spray can. According to the table of comparison, which spray can (1–5) is the least harmful for the environment?

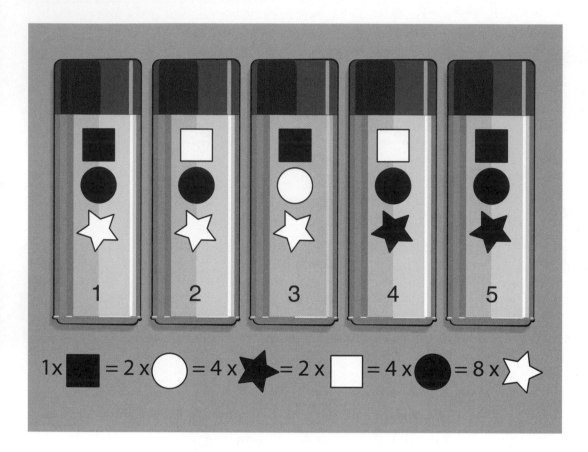

BLOCK ANAGRAM

Form the word that is described in the brackets with the letters above the grid. An extra letter is already in the right place.

TOASTER (board game for two players on a 10×10 square board)

★★★★ Color Blind by Teresa Lucchetti

ACROSS

1 Needling comment
5 Conductor Sir Georg
10 "Holy smoke!" of yore
14 Gaston's gal
15 "... above the fruited ___"
16 Strong inclination
17 Traditional English folk song?
19 Ball-___ hammer
20 Cleveland team
21 Duke's wife
23 Flop
24 Madame Bovary's lover
25 Birthplace of Camus
29 Ceaseless
32 Kind of code or graph
33 Titicaca's range
35 Extensive attack
36 Douay Bible book
38 "This I ___ see!"
40 Ranch unit
41 ___ a Letter to My Love (1981)
43 Diving places
45 Classic sneaker
46 Most extended
48 Gratifies
50 Genie offering
51 Three-time Hart Trophy winner
52 Arizona desert
55 Eavesdroppers?
59 Feminine suffix
60 Superhero with a power ring?
62 Stomp around and scream
63 Cornrow, for one
64 Crucifix letters
65 Warsaw Pact country
66 The Sandbox playwright
67 Tag info

DOWN

1 Adriatic resort
2 "Messiah" chorus
3 Lorna Doone hero John
4 Near
5 Shopaholic's problem
6 Guadalajara cheers
7 Washroom, briefly
8 In extra innings
9 Offend
10 Seventh heaven
11 Yahoos?
12 Space and Stone
13 Lion lairs
18 Linney in John Adams
22 Middling marks
25 Bubbling over
26 Catch, out West
27 Detroit team?
28 One way to become a parent
29 Bar legally
30 Achieve entente
31 W Yorkshire city
34 Third Army's WW2 area
37 Cal Tech grad
39 Parcel out
42 Put through the paces
44 Small finch
47 Mount Everest guide
49 Polar region with a "circle"
52 Andean land
53 Duck genus
54 Wooded hollow
55 Nastase of tennis
56 Emcee for NBC
57 Types a typo
58 Irritated condition
61 Smidgen

★ Zoo

All the words are hidden vertically, horizontally or diagonally—in both directions. The letters that remain unused form a sentence from left to right.

```
Z K A N W O O T S K O A L A K
O R S S O I R A R E A G R O E
T A I T N O L A L L I R O G L
T P A E P A B D A T P L S L I
E B A I C E K A E T O R T E D
R L C A X B U E B B T T O H O
K A N G A R O O S B E A R S C
L E I N O I L R R M A E K I O
H I P P O P O T A M U S S N R
L G O A S T N A L P L I S T C
L T H C I R T S O O K E E U P
A A N S I M A L H S I F O S A
M S I J A G U A R T H B R R C
A V E A T E W N E D A W I E I
T H E X T K I N C R L T K D R
I O N S M U I R A U Q A L I F
A E U Q A C A M F E A S E P A
N D S O U N L E R R I U Q S D
```

FISH
GORILLA
HAWK
HIPPOPOTAMUS
JAGUAR
KANGAROO
KOALA
LION
LLAMA
LOOK
MACAQUE
MARABOU
OSTRICH
OTTER
PARK
PLANTS
SEAL
SNAKES
SPIDERS
SQUIRREL
STORK
TROPICAL
VISITORS
WILDEBEEST

AFRICA	ASIA	BEARS
APES	BABOON	CROCODILE
AQUARIUM	BAT	ELK

DELETE ONE

Delete one letter from CORDIALLY PRESENT and find a rags-to-riches tale.

★★ Word Sudoku

Complete the grid so that each row, each column and each 3 x 3 frame contains the nine letters from the black box below. The hidden nine-letter word is in the diagonal from top left to bottom right.

A D E G I N O R U

	D		R		O		E	A
	G							N
		E	U					D
	N				G		A	
A	O				U		G	
R		G	A				U	
		O				I	R	
	I	E		G				U
		N						

UNCANNY TURN

Rearrange the letters of the phrase below to form a cognate anagram, one that is related or connected in meaning to the original phrase. The answer can be one or more words.

A HEALTHY DIET

★ Futoshiki

Fill in the 5 x 5 grid with the numbers from 1 to 5 once per row and column, while following the greater than/lesser than symbols shown. There is only one valid solution that can be reached through logic and clear thinking alone!

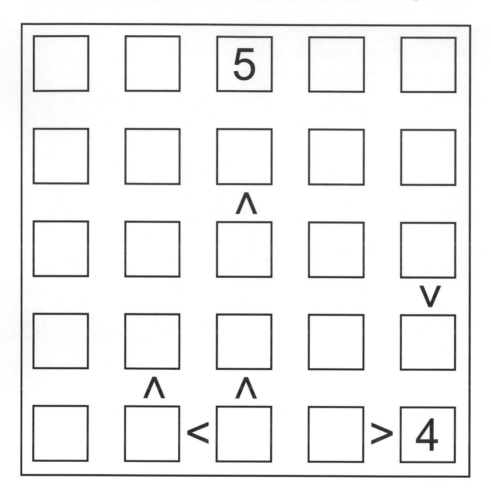

TRIANAGRAM

Three-word groups of anagrams are called triplets or trianagrams.
Complete the group:

B L A M I N G   _ _ _ _ _ _ _   _ _ _ _ _ _ _

★★★★ Hidden Forest by John M. Samson

ACROSS
1 Mast
5 First-stringers
10 Relief pitcher Sergio
14 Purplish
15 Luanda language
16 "___ so sorry"
17 Coat check*
19 Greek salad cheese
20 Pertains
21 Excited
23 "Give ___ while longer"
24 From scratch
25 Pianissimo, to a musician
29 Hits the hay after a long day*
32 Rough on the eyes
33 Tire asset
35 Share the load
36 Nabokov book
37 Ending for editor
38 Alabama's football rival
39 Become available, as a stock grant
41 Ferret relative
43 Dubai dignitary
44 Add to the value of
46 Corbin of *Psych*
48 Try to lighten up?
49 Lincoln center?
50 Run out on
53 Dessert option
57 Yurt
58 Quilled rodents*
60 Valentine material
61 Single entities
62 Sniggler's catch
63 Hot under the collar
64 "Common ___": Paine
65 "Everything must go" event

DOWN
1 Compassionate org.
2 Orange-juice option
3 *Rent-___* (1988)
4 TV genre
5 Informed
6 Resort near Santa Fe
7 Ambient music pioneer
8 They're pressed for cash
9 Colonel suspected of murder
10 Give a lift
11 Steamrolls*
12 Measure (out)
13 Mouthward
18 Small hawk
22 "Back ___ flash"
25 Worldly
26 "Candy is dandy" poet Nash
27 1983 Jennifer Beals film*
28 Done to death
29 Old Testament spy
30 Holmes novel ___ Venner
31 Rudely reject
34 Have a bite
40 Contaminated
41 Beatle gardener
42 Hermit
43 More than just rivals
45 Flanders of *The Simpsons*
47 Gather grain
50 Legendary Hun king, in saga
51 Wall Street pessimist
52 Zilch
53 Vaudeville lineup
54 Draft-eligible
55 Computer brand
56 Latin I verb
59 ___ Tin Tin

★ Horoscope

Fill in the grid so that every row, every column and every vertical frame of six boxes contains six different symbols: health, work, money, happiness, family and love. Look at the row or column that corresponds with your sign of the zodiac and find out which of the six symbols are important for you today. The symbols appear in increasing order of importance (1–6). It's up to you to translate the meaning of each symbol to your specific situation.

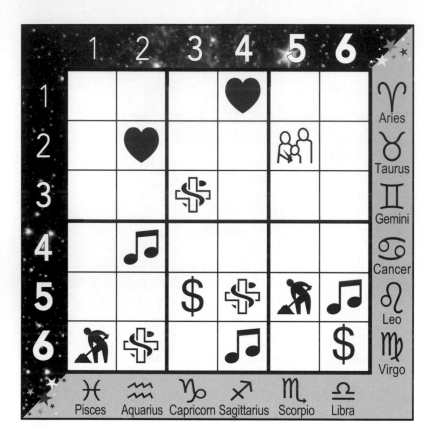

WORD WALL

Beginning at the left side of the wall, make a word by adding one group of letters from each column as you move left to right. When you have found the first word, go back to the second column and start the next word, gathering one group of letters from each column, and so on until all the letters are used to make six words.

★★ BrainSnack®—Time Gap

What time is it if you completely rotate the minute hand twice and then rotate the time scale of the clock 90° in the opposite direction?

LETTERBLOCKS

Move the letterblocks around so that words are formed on top and below that you can associate with courts. In some blocks, the letter from the top row has been switched with the letter from the bottom row.

I C E R D V O
E C T I V R D

★★★★ Historic Homes by Brian O'Shea

ACROSS

1 Animal that may charge
5 Ark's resting place?
11 Swimming distance
14 Sight from Bern
15 *American Psycho* is one
16 "... ___ reasonable facsimile"
17 Monticello resident
20 North African republic
21 Reveres
22 Some block boundaries: Abbr.
23 Think piece
24 Compactness
28 Painter Chagall
30 Guido's note
31 Old Persian Gulf kingdom
33 Computernik
37 *Hud* heroine
39 Opposition
40 *Sesame Street* Muppet
41 Property document
42 Puncture
43 Ending for human or planet
44 Miss Bond in *Casino Royale*
46 Bowmen
50 Sedate
53 Water under le pont
54 Female in a striped coat
57 Fatuous
61 Finca Vigia resident
63 Really big shoe
64 Layered
65 Fly off the handle
66 Letter addenda
67 Skunk's kin
68 River that begins in Nord

DOWN

1 "Bright Eyes" composer Mike
2 Pearl Harbor locale
3 Elvis ___ Presley
4 Neglectful
5 Join a surgical team
6 Sri Lankan king
7 Had, in a way
8 Hardly scarce
9 Expressions of puppy love?
10 Have trouble balancing
11 Forfeits
12 Wafting thing
13 Mammy Yokum
18 Bubbly wine
19 Bail out
24 Beyond tired
25 Fanning in *Super 8*
26 Handle
27 Shtetl gossip
28 Cobra's cousin
29 *High Noon* heroine
32 Grassland
34 Gin flavoring
35 Persian Gulf ruler
36 Fishing gear
38 Think the world of
39 Best-of-all ending
45 Christmas carol start
47 Live at
48 Marked man in Genesis
49 Half-starved
50 Like cliffs
51 Pirellis, e.g.
52 *Despicable Me* girl
55 Flap
56 Japheth and Ham's brother
57 Communicant's response
58 "___ only trying to help"
59 Main church area
60 Watchful one
62 Lincoln's *Cap'n* ___

★★★ Sudoku

Fill in the grid so that each row, each column and each 3 x 3 frame contains every number from 1 to 9.

	1	3		6	2	5		
	9		8				3	
4		6		5				2
		5			7	9		8
			4		8	7		
							1	
				4	9			
6	7		2					
								9

SYMBOL SUMS

Can you work out these number sums using three of these four symbols? **+ − ÷ ✕**
(No fractions or minus numbers are involved in the sum as you progress from left to right.)

$$64 \ \Box \ 8 \ \Box \ 8 \ \Box \ 11 = 18$$

★★ Number Cluster

Complete the grid by constituting adjoining clusters that consist of as many cubes as the number on the cubes. At cube 5, for instance, you will have to make a five-cube cluster. Two or more figure cubes of the same value belong to the same cluster. You can only place your cubes along horizontal and/or vertical lines.

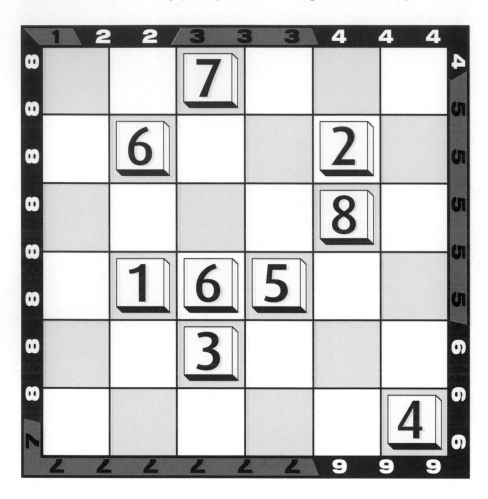

SANDWICH

What FOUR-letter word belongs between the word on the left and the word on the right, so that the first and second word, and the second and third word, each form a common compound word or phrase?

WHIP _ _ _ _ WASH

★★★★ Sitcom Pilots by John M. Samson

ACROSS
1 Tear gas
5 *Cheers* waitress
10 Kill a bill
14 Islands off Galway
15 "Like ___ in the headlights"
16 Novello in *Gosford Park*
17 A bit less than a meter
18 Crack under pressure
19 Washbowl
20 "Justice for All" sitcom
23 Greenwich Village campus
24 Society bud
25 Wisconsin team
29 Thunders
33 "A Sorta Fairytale" singer
34 Weaver and Monroe
36 Sound heard in a cave
37 State
38 It'll take your breath away
39 Yon maiden
40 Agendum ingredient
42 ___ ballerina
44 Crystal-baller
45 "Summer Wind" singer
47 Along in years
49 ___ polloi
50 Actress Barbara___ Geddes
51 "Most Chicks Won't Eat Veal" sitcom
59 Associate with
60 Minolta rival
61 Crumb
62 Shield shape, in heraldry
63 Daniilidou of tennis
64 Editor's annotation
65 Like certain sums
66 Former Alaskan capital
67 Use a whetstone

DOWN
1 Rudolph in *Bridesmaids*
2 Kazakhstan sea
3 Carlson of *The Simpsons*
4 ABC's *Happy* ___
5 Snag
6 Esau's wife
7 Russo in *Showtime*
8 Explorer Ericson
9 Teen haunts
10 Obvious to the eye
11 Insidious
12 Award for Marian Seldes
13 *Mork and Mindy* planet
21 Comical Louis
22 Gibson in *The Bounty*
25 Rationale
26 Stradivari's teacher
27 Senior diplomat
28 Native Israeli
29 What to put on Mame
30 Palette pigment
31 Potter's device
32 "I take it back"
35 French royalty
41 John of *Frasier*
42 Charles and Charming
43 Country on the Adriatic
44 Egocentric
46 Ode starter
48 Andrea ___ Sarto
51 Spelling or 33 Across
52 Feral
53 Droopy watch artist
54 *Without* ___ (Grateful Dead album)
55 Sound from a wild goose chase?
56 John P. Marquand sleuth
57 Berkshire school
58 Scruff
59 Write hastily

★★★ Concentration—Gridlock

Cut the grid into three identical pieces. The three pieces have the same shape and surface but can be turned and/or mirrored.

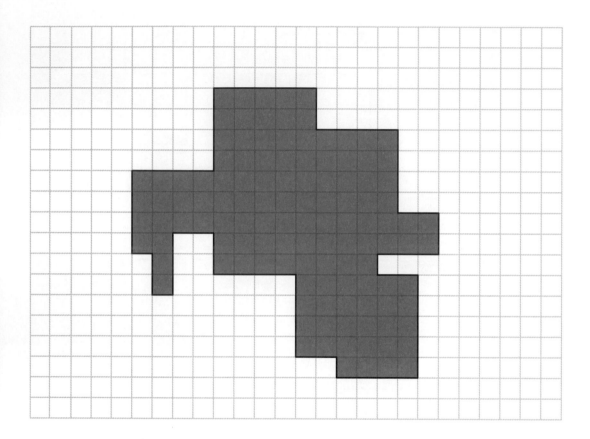

DOODLE PUZZLE

A doodle puzzle is a combination of images, letters and/or numbers that represent a word or a concept. If you cannot solve a doodle puzzle, do not look at the answer right away. Think hard—and outside the box.

★★★ BrainSnack®—On the Green

Where is a golf ball missing? Answer like this: C3.

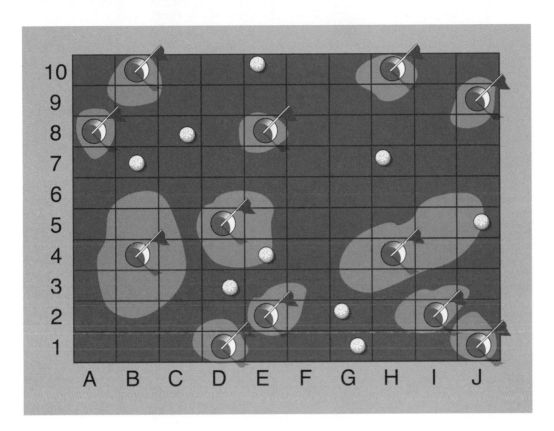

CLOCKWISE

The answers to the clues from 1 to 12 are all seven-letter words that end with the letter L. When you have solved the puzzle correctly, working clockwise from 1, the twelve letters in the outer circle will spell a word meaning "a name."

1 Arctic whale	7 Generous, abundant
2 Strange, eccentric	8 Of the south
3 Archangel	9 Lachrymose
4 Spanish Spanish	10 Lacking manners
5 Relating to marriage	11 Renaissance artist
6 Distrustful of human goodness	12 Stare at

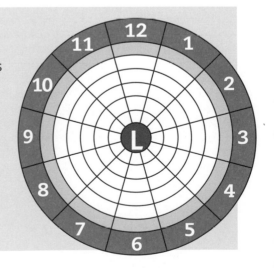

★★★★ TV Quotes by Kelly Lynch

ACROSS

1 Win for Magnus Carlsen
5 Gem measure
10 1994 baseball biopic
14 "I'd hate to break up ___"
15 *The Death of the Author* author
16 Chill factor?
17 "To the moon, Alice!" sitcom
20 Florida tribe
21 Indiana NBA team
22 "___ the pulse of summer": Dylan Thomas
23 Copier brand
24 Fruits of the vine
27 Not long ago
31 Sanctioned
32 Old Scratch
33 ___ Speedwagon
34 Taj Mahal site
35 Split hairs
36 "I ___ it!" (Skelton catch phrase)
37 Arctic explorer
38 Mall draws
39 "You Light Up My Life" singer
40 Fire and water
42 Force
43 Sports schedule column
44 Draped wear of Delhi
45 Put on Broadway
48 Prude
52 "Come on down!" game show
54 "Now I Know" singer White
55 Quickly
56 *Little Shop of Horrors* role
57 Member of the Winnebago nation
58 Entitled
59 Leningrad's river

DOWN

1 Gets all tangled
2 1982 Davis Cup captain
3 Overbrim with
4 Addis Ababa locale
5 Birchbark watercraft
6 "Chasing Pavements" singer
7 "One Boy, One Girl" singer Collin
8 Use a crosshair
9 Kind of storm
10 *Moulin Rouge* dance
11 Arched molding
12 *Perry Mason* star Raymond
13 Nancy Drew's friend
18 Dawn
19 Like Cheerios
23 Jupiter moon
24 "Daggers" look
25 Monarchial
26 Go together
27 Utters in a frenzy
28 Band
29 Sierra ___
30 Call in the Alps
32 Like seawater
35 Alex Trebek, by birth
36 Realm
38 Ed Norton's workplace
39 Hole maker
41 Noisy bird
42 Brought about
44 Golf goof
45 Town WSW of Caen
46 "Can you beat ___?"
47 Windows 7 interface
48 Grin broadly
49 Tough boss
50 Knife, slangily
51 Landmark in Sicily
53 Bean counter

★ Sleep

All the words are hidden vertically, horizontally or diagonally—in both directions. The letters that remain unused form a sentence from left to right.

```
E  S  P  L  E  N  E  U  R  O  N  S  T  E  P
A  O  I  U  S  N  O  R  E  I  S  A  S  Y  W
R  T  B  A  R  S  Y  T  T  O  S  P  E  T  R
L  E  O  S  T  E  E  H  C  T  E  R  I  T
Y  K  H  K  C  E  V  N  B  G  O  D  Y  T  B
E  N  R  C  S  U  Y  O  L  A  I  D  U  N  S
E  A  G  E  N  S  R  M  C  U  E  N  X  A  H
D  L  R  A  O  L  S  E  O  E  F  U  S  U  T
O  B  U  C  O  Y  E  S  P  R  I  E  O  Q  N
Z  T  M  N  Z  E  T  T  E  S  N  W  K  I  P
E  U  B  W  E  L  S  I  H  R  H  I  L  A  P
O  C  L  A  H  Y  S  A  V  A  T  E  N  I  W
F  K  E  Y  A  C  A  L  E  I  R  T  E  G  L
F  I  Y  L  W  R  E  A  K  R  T  G  A  T  Y
O  N  A  U  D  R  E  A  M  S  C  C  I  M  R
B  R  M  E  L  A  T  O  N  I  N  E  A  C  O
M  D  Y  I  N  T  H  E  L  O  B  E  D  N  N
G  R  U  M  E  T  A  B  O  L  I  S  M  N  I
```

DREAMS
EARLY
GRUMBLE
INACTIVITY
LETHARGIC
MATTRESS
MELATONIN
METABOLISM
MORNING
NAP
NEURONS
NIGHT
OBSCURE
QUANTITY
REST
RISE
SHEET
SNOOZE
SNORE
TUCK IN
WAKEFULNESS
YAWN

ALARM
BED
BLANKET

COSY
COVER UP
DARK

DECREASE
DEEP
DOZE OFF

FRIENDS?

What do the following words have in common?

AWE TWO HAND BOTHER WHOLE TIRE WIN

★★★ Sudoku X

Fill in the grid so that each row, each column and each 3 x 3 frame contains every number from 1 to 9. The two main diagonals of the grid also contain every number from 1 to 9.

				4				
			7	3		4	9	6
	6					7	1	
	1	5			4		2	
7	9				5		4	
		8		2		1		
	3				7		6	
		1			3			

BLOCK ANAGRAM

Form the word that is described in the brackets with the letters above the grid. An extra letter is already in the right place.

SOLAR TIE *(played by one person)*

						I		

★★★ The Simpsons by Kelly Lynch

ACROSS

1 Cowardly Lion actor
5 Raiderettes' shout
10 Dutch cheese
14 "You can't pray ___"
15 Sight along the Mississippi
16 Prefix for circle
17 The Simpsons' next-door neighbor
19 Ice star Michelle
20 Medical school study
21 One hearing a confession
23 Sat in a cellar?
24 Spacious
25 Some Buffalo wings
28 Balloon baskets
31 Gather over time
32 Elbow-bender
33 Young Darth
34 Basketballer Bryant
35 Frost poem "___ Walk"
36 Saskatchewan lake
37 Nevada city
38 Diminish
39 Links legend Ben
40 Grapefruit units
42 Andalusian address
43 French bread?
44 Makes calls
45 It may be one-way
47 Battle of Tours locale
51 Baseball's Infante
52 Springfield tavern owner
54 Kunis of *Family Guy*
55 "Tomorrow" musical
56 Kipling's "Rikki-Tikki-___"
57 Roddick or Rooney
58 Burdened
59 Ride down a snowbank

DOWN

1 Pie crust ingredient
2 His, in Paris
3 Long-running plays
4 Prepare for a performance
5 "Yours truly" and others
6 Chopped down
7 12/24 and 12/31
8 Constantly, to Keats
9 Answer
10 Yupik speaker
11 Lisa Simpson's music teacher
12 Amo, ___, amat
13 Catnip cousin
18 Beeper calls
22 Took a horse
24 Paperboy's path
25 "Land ___!"

26 Whac-___ (arcade game)
27 Maggie Simpson's archenemy
28 What kids grow up to be
29 Lend ___ (listen)
30 St. Catherine's city
32 Bed supports
35 Not standard
36 Is made up (of)
38 Prefix for space
39 Whopping
41 2012 U.S. Open winner
42 Expropriated
44 O'Grady of song
45 Home of Monet's "Water Lilies"
46 "Not folding"
47 Await a decision

48 Israeli airline
49 Fly off the handle
50 Spin out
53 Three ___ match

★★ Maze—Beehive

Enter the beehive where indicated, pass through all the cells with honey once, then exit where indicated.

SANDWICH

What five-letter word belongs between the word on the left and the word on the right, so that the first and second word, and the second and third word, each form a common compound word or phrase?

WAR _ _ _ _ _ RACE

★★★ Sport Maze

Draw the shortest way from the ball to the goal. You can only move along vertical and horizontal lines, not along diagonal lines. The figure on each square indicates the number of squares the ball must be moved in the same direction. You can change direction at each stop.

3	1	4	4	3	2
3	2	4	4	1	5
5	1	3	3	1	5
4	1	2		3	2
4	2	1	4	1	1
3	3	1	5	2	3

ONE LETTER LESS OR MORE

The word on the right side contains the letters of the word on the left side plus or minus the letter in the middle. One letter is already in the right place.

S T U R G E O N +Y ☐ ☐ ☐ N ☐ ☐ ☐ ☐

★★★ BrainSnack®—Slippery

Which color (1–5) should replace the question mark on the skin of the snake?

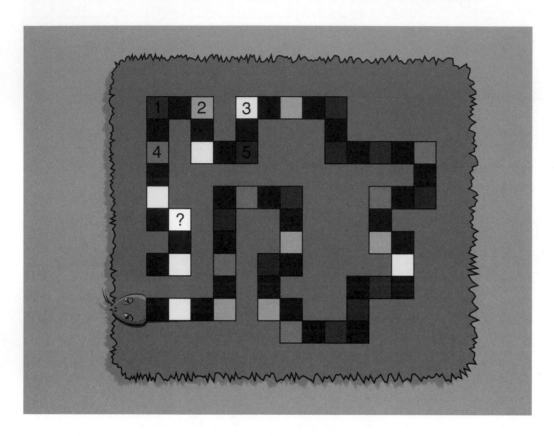

LETTER LINE

Put a letter in each of the squares below to make a word that describes "a light effect." The number clues refer to other words that can be made from the whole.

9 5 6 10 4 8 SNUGGLE CLOSE; 6 10 3 2 4 5 INTEGRAL PART, PRINCIPAL; 3 2 1 6 10 4 5 ONE SENT ON A MISSION; 6 2 4 5 5 9 PEEVISHNESS, ILL HUMOR; 3 9 10 5 4 1 2 5 GRACEFUL MAMMAL; 8 3 6 8 4 ARTIST'S FRAME

1	2	3	4	5	6	7	8	9	10

★★★★★ B as in ... by Tim Wagner

ACROSS

1 Cowshed
5 Lord's estate
10 *East of Eden* heroine
14 Baseball brothers
15 Forearm bones
16 Post bond
17 San Francisco harbor pilots?
19 Po tributary
20 Heart
21 Parade watcher, often
23 "Too-Ra-Loo-Ra-Loo-___"
24 "500" race
25 Argued politics
29 Gifted Harvard
32 Hebrew month
33 Baseball commissioner Bud
35 Early Japanese capital
36 City in Baden-Württemberg
37 Help out
38 Sign of a beer fan
39 Comics pub patron
41 Practiced a trade
43 "Fat chance"
44 Mukluk wearers
46 Turns over a new leaf
48 "___ no respect!": Dangerfield
49 Service charge
50 Across-the-board
53 Mailing out
57 Dog food brand
58 Horse or camel, e.g.?
60 Ex of Tiger Woods
61 Two drinks, for some
62 El ___ (weather phenomenon)
63 Marvin and Majors
64 Brockovich et al.
65 Nibble

DOWN

1 Paul Bunyan's ox
2 "Ah, me!"
3 Rogers and Clark
4 IV or VI
5 Iron pumper's pride
6 Der ___ (Adenauer)
7 Florida-to-Maine dir.
8 Propellers of a sort
9 Relaxing
10 Walk out on
11 Police transport for no-goodniks?
12 Space Mountain, e.g.
13 Dragonfly wings
18 Surgeon's subj.
22 Plus
25 Two-spot
26 Fitzgerald and Raines
27 Country-cookin' dessert?

28 Distributes cards
29 Pillow stuffing
30 Blow a fuse
31 eHarmony connections
34 2018 Super Bowl
40 Easy marks
41 Drink
42 Vanquishes
43 Crying out for
45 Saint-Tropez sea
47 Sean in *Milk*
50 Tennis pro Monfils
51 Fashion magazine
52 Place to hole up
53 Dermatologist's concern
54 Keith Urban song
55 Governess
56 Shine brightly
59 Caesar's 901

★★★ Word Sudoku

Complete the grid so that each row, each column and each 3 x 3 frame contains the nine letters from the black box below. The hidden nine-letter word is in the diagonal from top left to bottom right.

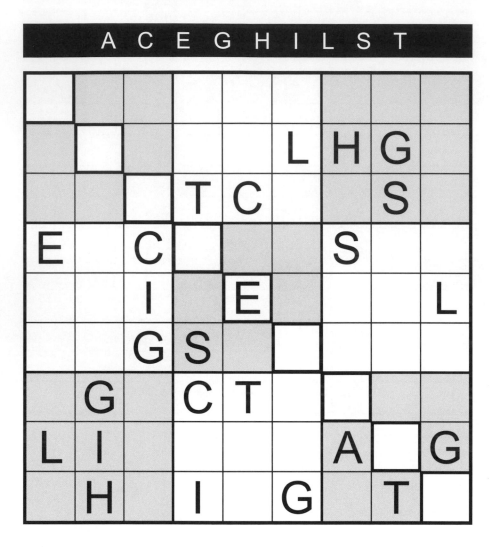

A C E G H I L S T

THREE-IN-ONE

Using all of the letters listed below only once, can you find the names of three long-running Broadway musicals?

a a b c c c d e e e g h i i i k l l m o r s s s w

★ Kakuro

Each number in a black area is the sum of the numbers that you have to enter in the next empty boxes. The empty boxes that make up the sum are called a run. The sum of the across run is written above the diagonal in the black area and the sum of the down run is written below the diagonal. Runs can only contain the numbers 1 through 9 and each number in a run can only be used once. The gray boxes only contain odd numbers and the white only even numbers.

DOUBLETALK

Homophones are words that share the same pronunciation, no matter how they are spelled. If they are spelled differently then they are called heterographs. Find heterographs meaning:

PASSED THROUGH THE AIR and CURRENT-DIRECTING PASSAGEWAY

★★★★★ Bank Holiday by John M. Samson

ACROSS

1 A Simpson
5 Spot of tea?
10 Aardvark's dinner
14 Esau's wife
15 Steep slide
16 Whitecap feature
17 Bank vaults?
19 Visage
20 May birthstone
21 Embassy member
23 SOS response
24 Noncleric
25 Called back to work
29 Crash site?
32 Word from the pews
33 Some stadiums
35 "Certainly!"
36 Christian denom.
37 ___-di-dah
38 Seasonal libation
39 Danson and Turner
41 Starters, in sports
43 Volcano near Messina
44 "O Canada" et al.
46 "Everybody's Talkin'"
   singer
48 Currency since 1999
49 Like Babe Ruth's no.
50 Spear carrier
53 National game of
   India
57 Spellbind
58 Payments to the
   coroner?
60 Away from the wind
61 Island loop
62 Enlarge a hole
63 Teri in Oh, God!
64 Makeup maven Lauder
65 Erstwhile air fleet

DOWN

1 Low-down
2 Painter Elsheimer
3 Pearl Harbor hero
4 "___ in Spain stays
   ..."
5 Dressed down
6 Landing sound
7 Salzburg locale: Abbr.
8 Willow tree
9 Cuddles
10 Flings
11 Worthless IRAs?
12 RPM gauge
13 Peter Pan pirate
18 Samson's source of
   strength
22 Wee lad
25 Jamaican sectarian
26 German seaport

27 Comfort station ATM?
28 Dunces
29 Borstal Boy author
30 Maine college town
31 Mullally of Will &
   Grace
34 West in My Little
   Chickadee
40 React fearfully
41 One-celled organisms
42 Wonderwork
43 Rolle and Ralston
45 Assam silkworm
47 Nobelist Walesa
50 Chase flies
51 Judge Dredd villain
   Blint
52 Spoils
53 Greene's "quiet
   American"

54 Cools with cubes
55 3-person card game
56 Doctrines
59 Dash's cousin.

★ Sudoku Twin

Fill in the grid so that each row, each column and each 3 x 3 frame contains every number from 1 to 9. A sudoku twin is two connected 9 x 9 sudokus.

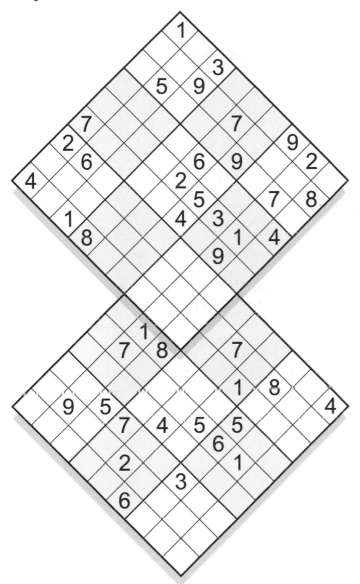

TRIANAGRAM

Three-word groups of anagrams are called triplets or trianagrams.
Complete the group:

TROPES   _ _ _ _ _ _   _ _ _ _ _ _

★★★ BrainSnack®—Pot Luck

Which letter should replace the question mark?

QUICK CROSSWORD

Place the words associated with films listed below in the crossword grid.

ACT CLIP EDITOR EPIC FAST FLIP FOCUS IRIS LIP LOOP MIX MUTE OFF SET

★★★★★ Pick a Number by Kelly Lynch

ACROSS

1 "___ Otis Regrets": Porter
5 Makes presents presentable
10 Young newts
14 Minuscule bit
15 Path through seats
16 They lead to mi
17 Number of world time zones
19 Trinity College library architect
20 Trig function
21 Quieted with Quaalude
23 One for Monet
24 Less than a little
25 Superlative for Atlanta Airport
29 Most challenging
32 "___ you forgetting something?"
33 Endure
35 Wall St. newcomer
36 Word processor command
37 Peerless
38 Id counterparts
39 Suffix for serpent
40 Taos building material
41 Muslim messiah
42 Doom
44 Less drawn-out
46 Hatcher of *Lois & Clark*
47 New England cape
48 Stay away from
51 Clothed
55 Museo del Prado display
56 Number of Old Testament books
58 In stitches
59 Kafkaesque
60 Scandalous suffix
61 TV schedule position
62 Prevent
63 Pung or coaster

DOWN

1 Catcher's glove
2 Landlocked state
3 Compact Chevy pickup
4 Ruddy, as a complexion
5 ___ *World* (1992)
6 Diplomacy breakdown
7 Kyushu volcano
8 Appealing addition
9 Play to the balcony
10 "The Black Prince"
11 Number of teaspoons in a cup
12 Locust, for one
13 Email
18 Religious dogma
22 Risk
25 Fundamental

26 Heavenly prefix
27 Number of points in one inch
28 Condor claw
29 *Tap* star Gregory
30 Fine china
31 Lulu's "___, With Love"
34 Sportscaster Costas
37 Fessed up
38 Salary
40 Designed for flying
41 Python or Woolley
43 Dressed
45 "Mad" Depp role
48 Game fish
49 City on the Oka River
50 The old "you"
51 Indy driver Luyendyk

52 Coin of Iran
53 German duck
54 Quitclaim
57 NYC's first subway line

★ Swimming

All the words are hidden vertically, horizontally or diagonally—in both directions. The letters that remain unused form a sentence from left to right.

```
S S G O G G L E S E E S C D W
C I G M P M I G N K N L O I G
U D F E I M N D O S S I N S E
B R E E L I U R N N P D D T A
I O A S N R T J O N L E I A R
C C R I A S A I O F U V T N E
L E A N K S T S L E N D I C S
E R C C H A S O M R G R O E C
T E A O E E A Y S R E A N R U
H B W R L T E H A L A O A E E
T E C H O Y A E V I D B M T N
R E F O O M R M O F R G O A I
R C O M P E T I T I O N L W R
Y E C O R E A T K I O I P N O
O B O E C B A U S C E V I I L
U T U S E O S A L M U I D O H
N S T E V M L A N E E D R Y C
G M U S C B L E K R O N S L E
```

DIVE
DIVING BOARD
DUCK
ENDURANCE
FEAR
FLOAT
GOGGLES
JUMP
LANE
LEGS
LESSON
PLUNGE
POOL
RECORD
RECREATION
RESCUE
SHAMPOO
SHOWER
SLIDE
SNORKEL
TRAINING
WATER
YOUNG

ARMS
BACKSTROKE
BOMB

CHLORINE
COMPETITION
CONDITION

CUBICLE
DIPLOMA
DISTANCE

DOUBLETALK

Homophones are words that share the same pronunciation, no matter how they are spelled. If they are spelled differently then they are called heterographs. Find heterographs meaning:

A GOOD TIME and TO CRY LOUDLY

★★ Do the Math

Enter numbers in each row and column to arrive at the end totals. Only numbers 1–9 are used and only once.

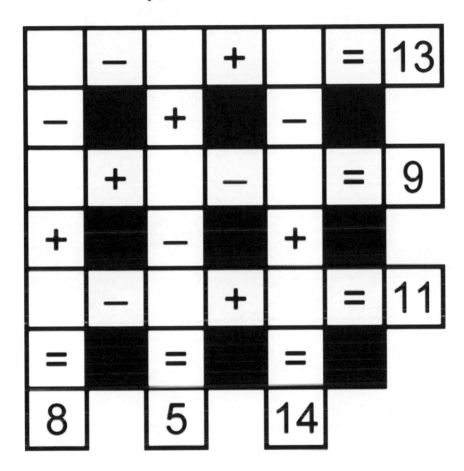

LETTERBLOCKS

Move the letterblocks around so that words are formed on top and below that you can associate with fast food. In some blocks, the letter from the top row has been switched with the letter from the bottom row.

★★★★★ Placement Test by Teresa Lucchetti

ACROSS

1 Emerald City architect
5 Subway in Paris
10 Oasis fruit
14 Part of a hocus-pocus phrase
15 Be of assistance
16 Geraint's love
17 T
20 Lettering aid
21 Amplify
22 Mauna ___
23 People with their pants on fire?
24 Bloody Mary ingredient
28 Indigo-yielding shrub
30 Schoenberg's *Moses und* ___
31 Sturdy chiffon
33 Half a dance
36 OA
40 "What'd I ___?": Rare Earth
41 He uses the Palmer method?
42 "The South-Sea House" essayist
43 Hosea in the Douay
44 Metallic gray
47 Suit to the circumstances
50 Formerly named
51 Ahab's weapon
54 Peter Pan player, often
58 N
60 Summer quaffs
61 Clay pigment
62 Naysayer
63 Unit of force
64 Palustrine plants
65 In the event that

DOWN

1 *Chicken Run* chicken
2 Help a hood
3 Excite
4 China, by and large
5 #1 song from *Flashdance*
6 The Dark Side
7 Khaki shade
8 Diana in *The Hospital*
9 Swan genus
10 Intense auto cleaning
11 *The Pilot's Wife* author Shreve
12 Clock of a sort
13 Idyllic places
18 Noncoms
19 Margay, for one
24 Lassie's lids
25 *Fidelio* solo
26 Factor in a wine review
27 Hiking cue
28 Builds a pot
29 Drama with choral chants
32 "___ were you ..."
33 Merry old king
34 *Aquarius* musical
35 "___ in the Life of a Fool"
37 Simon's ___ the Red Hot Lovers
38 Previous to
39 Flip-flop
43 Stand against
45 Provokes
46 Nullified tennis serves
47 Up on the count
48 Gallant
49 *As You Like It* forest
52 Pervasive smell
53 Perfectly agreeable
54 Played a winner
55 Hamburg article
56 A.A. candidates
57 Agitated state
59 This miss

★★★★ Futoshiki

Fill in the 5 x 5 grid with the numbers from 1 to 5 once per row and column, while following the greater than/lesser than symbols shown. There is only one valid solution that can be reached through logic and clear thinking alone!

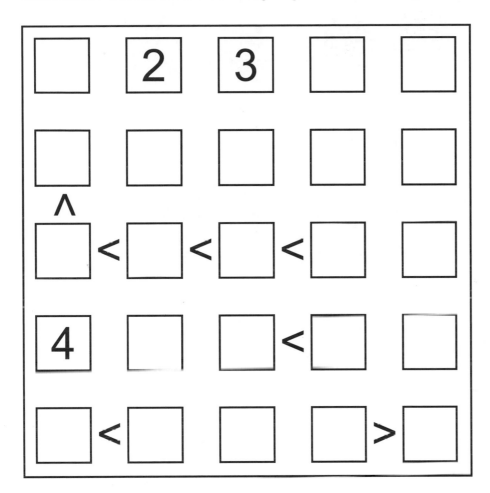

CHANGELINGS

Each of the three lines of letters below spell the names of types of tall buildings, but the letters have been mixed up. Four letters from the first word are now in the third line, four letters from the third word are in the second line and four letters from the second word are in the first line. The remaining letters are in their original places. What are the words?

L I Y H S H O P S R
S K L C C R A K E W
C G O T U T O E E R

★★★ BrainSnack®—Odd Block

Which group of blocks (1–6) does not belong?

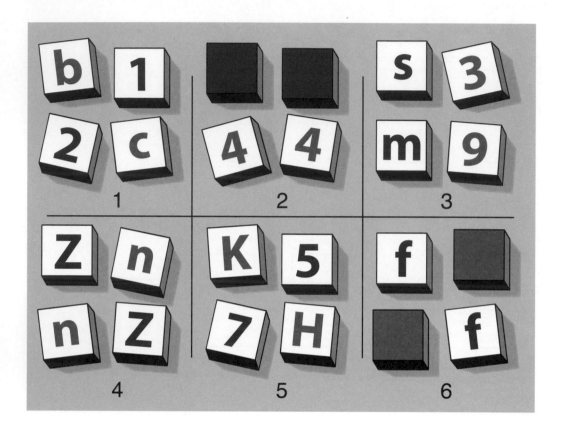

QUICK WORD SEARCH

Find the words related to vacations in the word search grid.

```
T  R  A  I  L  Z  M  R  H  L  A  K  E  L  K
R  I  F  H  C  A  E  B  O  O  K  C  V  E  A
U  U  S  A  P  L  A  N  E  O  T  D  A  T  E
N  F  M  I  A  T  S  A  O  C  M  E  E  O  R
K  P  C  X  V  P  H  O  T  O  U  R  L  M  B
```

BEACH BOOK BREAK CAMP COAST DATE FUN HOTEL LAKE LEAVE MAP
MOTEL PHOTO PLAN PLANE RELAX ROOM TOUR TRAIL TRUNK VISIT

★★★★★ Playing the Market by Linda Lather

ACROSS
1 Mine, to madame
5 Trick-or-treater
10 Type of socks
14 *Doctor Faustus* novelist
15 Luminous radiations
16 Jesus's grandfather
17 Securities that rise in value, e.g.?
20 Cookware item
21 "Send in the Clowns" singer
22 Landon of politics
23 It goes to the swiftest
24 Unprofessional one
28 Evidence of a bad paint job
31 Level, in London
32 Nigeria's largest city
34 Overpower
35 General Mandible, for one
36 E Indian lentil dish
37 Dastardly Amin
38 Charlie Parker's sobriquet
40 Land south of Sicily
42 Cathedral cross
43 Two-wheeled vehicle
45 Thurible smoke
47 *Cheers* accountant
48 *This Is Spinal ___* (1984)
49 Fables
52 Holden in *Network*
56 What brokerage consultants possess?
58 Square footage
59 Regal wear
60 Heat or Magic
61 Aquatic bird
62 Riverine mammal
63 Saarinen of Gateway Arch fame

DOWN
1 Sound boosters
2 Academic grade
3 "Tell me ___ haven't heard"
4 Enlarge, in a way
5 "Watch your back"
6 Wounded
7 Furor
8 Diane in *American Cowslip*
9 Arabian an Gibson
10 Menu listings
11 Diversion
12 Sommer in *A Shot in the Dark*
13 Knowing
18 Palindromic magazine title
19 Russian ruler
24 Most Semites
25 Crazily happy
26 Copernicus, notably
27 O'Reilly of *M*A*S*H*
28 Chicago Symphony conductor (1969–91)
29 Honors
30 A bit nasty
33 Hoedown participant
39 Entrance-level job?
40 Keepsake
41 Advocating peace
42 Abundantly filled
44 Lounge group, often
46 Ring up
49 Jazz singing
50 Ran full tilt
51 Burlesque piece
52 "She ___ a Yellow Ribbon"
53 Nice thought
54 John in *Johnny Reno*
55 In-basket item
57 D.C. baseballer

★★ Find the Right Word

Knowing that every arrow points to a letter and that no letter can touch another vertically, horizontally or diagonally, find the missing letters that form a keyword in reading direction. A letter cannot be located on an arrow. We show one letter in a circle to help you get started.

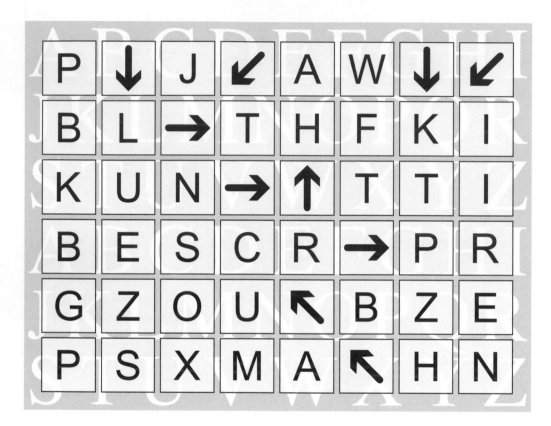

CHANGELINGS

Each of the three lines of letters below spell the names of objects associated with the bathroom, but the letters have been mixed up. Four letters from the first word are now in the third line, four letters from the third word are in the second line and four letters from the second word are in the first line. The remaining letters are in their original places. What are the words?

```
T B O T L B E T S H
B U F B S A B A V H
A O T E R H H R U E
```

★ Word Ladders

Convert the word at the top of the ladders into the word at the bottom, using all the rungs in between. On each rung, you must put a valid word that has the same letters as the word above it, apart from one letter change. There may be more than one way of achieving this.

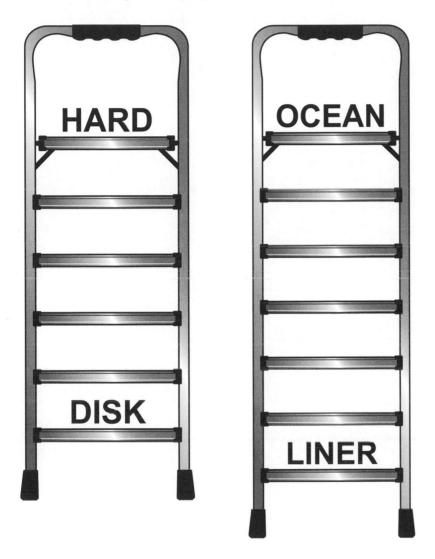

TRIANAGRAM

Three-word groups of anagrams are called triplets or trianagrams.
Complete the group:

P A I N T E R _ _ _ _ _ _ _   _ _ _ _ _ _ _

★★★ Sudoku

Fill in the grid so that each row, each column and each 3 x 3 frame contains every number from 1 to 9.

							1	
				4				6
	8	9						
					5	6		7
	7				8	2	4	
			4		6			
		1		3				
5	4		7		1			
6	9	7						4

SYMBOL SUMS

Can you work out these number sums using three of these four symbols? **+ − ÷ ×**
(No fractions or minus numbers are involved in the sum as you progress from left to right.)

1 ☐ 23 ☐ 7 ☐ 4 = 4

★★★★★ C- by Mary Leonard

ACROSS
1 Lamp replacement
5 Leave open-mouthed
10 Sine field
14 Hebrew prophet in the Douay Bible
15 Waif
16 Produce dividends
17 Jack Sprat's lifestyle?
19 Father of the Edomites
20 Thwarts
21 Threads
23 Govt. loan backer
24 Tina's *30 Rock* costar
25 Fun-run handouts
29 Smartphone platform
32 Israeli vacation spot
33 Striped antelope
35 "No prob!"
36 Humpback's kin
37 NYC subway line
38 Leibman or Ely
39 Active span
41 Of the eye
43 HR Dept. data
44 Seems
46 Kind of lantern
48 Oklahoma city
49 *Songs ___ Minor*: Keys album
50 Significant other
53 Diary entries, maybe
57 Bologna bear
58 Like prostrate snoozers?
60 Koh-i-___ diamond
61 Join the club
62 Morales in *La Bamba*
63 Syndicate heads
64 Table mat
65 Move suddenly

DOWN
1 Dauntless
2 Suit beneficiary
3 Canadian flag image
4 Work for
5 Turn in the wash
6 Dallas team, to fans
7 French for "friend"
8 Bluish white metal
9 Isle of Wight locale
10 Wobbles
11 Extreme BMX racing track?
12 Latin hymn "Dies ___"
13 Safari sights
18 Bert in a lion suit
22 Secondhand
25 Seed coat
26 Hypnotist's command
27 Coiffeur, e.g.?
28 Freudian mistakes
29 Marx Brothers bit
30 Clubs with bladelike heads
31 Close-grained
34 Word with collection or critic
40 Gurus
41 Talked while the waiter wrote
42 For the most part
43 Knotted up
45 "You Will Be My ___ True Love"
47 Andean ancient
50 Home for some lilies
51 Ending for buck
52 Nevada border city
53 Short-runway craft
54 *La Storia* novelist Morante
55 Glum drop
56 Fit of anger
59 ___ Lanka

★★ Maze—Traffic Grid

Enter the traffic grid, pass over all signposts from behind and then exit. You may not pass through a grid space more than once, and may not enter a grid space in the line of a signpost you have not yet passed over.

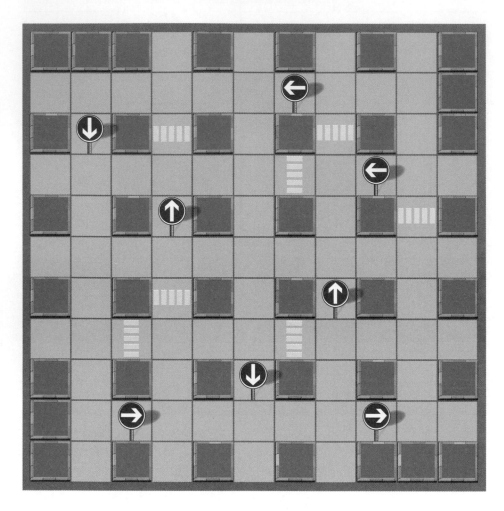

FRIENDS?

What do the following words have in common?

LATE PLANT ATLANTIC FORM PORT

★★★ BrainSnack®—Stack 'em

Where (1–3) should stack A or B be placed? Answer like this: 1B.

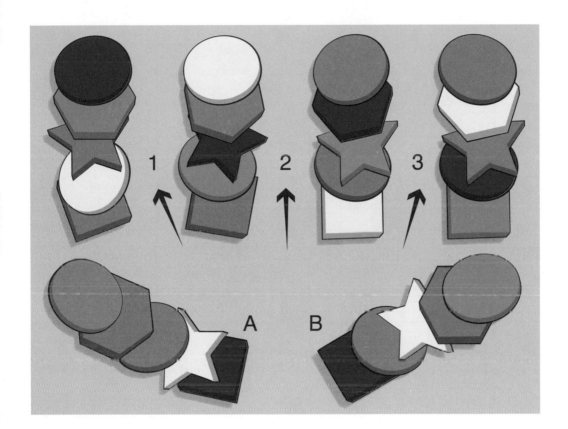

DOODLE PUZZLE

A doodle puzzle is a combination of images, letters and/or numbers that represent a word or a concept. If you cannot solve a doodle puzzle, do not look at the answer right away. Think hard—and outside the box.

★★★★★ F- by Mary Leonard

ACROSS

1 Alaimo of *Star Trek: DS9*
5 Air pollutants
10 "___ Lucky Old Sun"
14 Hawaiian food fish
15 Pontiff's vestment
16 He said "Fear is the path to the dark side"
17 ___ spell (relax)
18 Kissed off?
20 Archipelago off Scotland
22 Saucerful?
23 Knot up
24 Long-necked swimmer
25 Like many shorelines
27 Decorative glitter
31 Celebrates
32 Santa Claus has one
33 NAFTA counterpart
34 Grandstand sounds
35 Took testimony from
36 Corona
37 Summer in Le Havre
38 Austrian dessert
39 Debussy opus
40 Mastroianni in *La Dolce Vita*
42 See 36 Down
43 Halfpint around Mayberry
44 Clean energy
45 Looked into
48 Rain lightly
51 Favorable conditions for ballooning?
53 He played Grandpa Walton
54 Spike the punch
55 "___ So Vain": Simon
56 Shoshone tribesmen
57 Hefty slice
58 Sings an aria
59 Latin I verb

DOWN

1 Concert pit
2 Cap-___ (from head to foot)
3 What Cain turned out to be?
4 Pantomime game
5 Threw in a hand
6 Angel of the south wind
7 Vacation-planning aids
8 Hop-o'-my-thumb
9 *The Fugitive* actress
10 Key task?
11 One of Pandora's finds
12 "Pirate Alley" gulf
13 Youngsters
19 Chan portrayer
21 *Concord Sonata* composer
24 Easily lend
25 Violinist Zimbalist
26 Gaucho's lariat
27 "From ___ shining ..."
28 Meadowlands stores?
29 Ensnared elvers
30 Sudden-death ender
32 "Uncle Miltie"
35 Getaway occasions
36 Fulmination
38 Native American home
39 Taylor of *Factotum*
41 Halloween hang-up
42 Callie on *Grey's Anatomy*
44 Dum spiro ___ ("While I breathe, I hope")
45 Buddies
46 Iranian coin
47 Willy in *Free Willy*
48 Temple
49 Barrel-bottom residue
50 Irish Gaelic
52 Furthermore

★ Fencing

All the words are hidden vertically, horizontally or diagonally—in both directions. The letters that remain unused form a sentence from left to right.

```
F N O P A E W O E N G C T L L
I N R C R G D I P N S A I I U
I M E O O O D R I P E K H O N
N S M N C R T N A N O S S F G
S T I T P L I E P G H N O A E
T Y S A I A O O C C R O E T M
R L E C R H T A T T A T N B
U E R T G E Q O H W I B U O T
C I T R E S C A O I L O D C T
T H O R S A B R E A N Y N O M
O P A B E I K N D A C G U T K
R L R M I A E E O O N C O C F
P I Y I P H T N R Y H S A S I
C A J M O I A D G É L T W A N
D B S U P R O M P A T O T D C
R L A T D I I N E A R G I U L
C E Q U A G C T L D I D T E U
S L A N I F E S Y I E S E L B
```

EN GARDE
FINALS
FOIL
FOOTWORK
GARDE
GRIP
HIT
INSTRUCTOR
JUDGE
LUNGE
MASK
OLYMPICS
OPPONENT
PLIABLE
PRIORITY
PROTECTION
REMISE
RETREAT
ROMP
SABRE
STYLE
SWORD
TOUCHÉ
TRAINING
WEAPON

ATTACK
BLADE
BODY CORD

CHAMPION
CLOTHING
CLUB

COACH
CONTACT
DUEL

SANDWICH

What four-letter word belongs between the word on the left and the word on the right, so that the first and second word, and the second and third word, each form a common compound word or phrase?

SONG _ _ _ _ CAGE

★★★ Sport Maze

Draw the shortest way from the ball to the goal. You can only move along vertical and horizontal lines, not along diagonal lines. The figure on each square indicates the number of squares the ball must be moved in the same direction. You can change direction at each stop.

4	3	3	3	1	4
2	3	4	3	3	2
2	2	1	0	(1)	1
3	3	3	3	3	3
5	3	3	1	4	5
5	○	4	3	2	4

BLOCK ANAGRAM

Form the words that are described in the brackets with the letters above the grid. Extra letters are already in the right place.

KOREAN DOG *(largest marsupial of Australia)*

R				A				

★★★★★ World Clock I by John M. Samson

ACROSS

1 Heifers
5 Birthplace of Pythagoras
10 Large amount
14 Fail to name
15 At the ready
16 Five-sided plate
17 When it's noon in New York, it's 5:00 PM in ___
19 Mayberry resident
20 Wearing
21 When it's noon in Boston, it's 6:00 PM in ___
23 Place to park
24 Censure
25 Thought the world of
29 Biblical patriarch
32 Jeer
33 Dagwood's dog
35 California valley
36 Raggedy doll
37 Lit. submissions
38 Squelch
39 Memorization method
41 Arrives
43 Land of the Incas
44 "You wish!"
46 Nasty rulers
48 Pack in
49 Sun over Seville
50 Pulpit locale
53 When it's noon in Honolulu, it's 7:00 AM in ___
57 Flaubert's father
58 When it's noon in London, it's 1:00 PM in ___
60 "Twelve o'clock and ___ well"
61 Hajji's religion
62 Skating star Kulik
63 Cup of tea
64 Musician's skill
65 American-born Jordanian queen

DOWN

1 Crisp of baseball
2 Saudi Arabia neighbor
3 Sapient
4 Like a moonless sky
5 Greeted a captain
6 "What a pity!"
7 Sadie Hawkins Day catches
8 Dangerous whale
9 Broadway understudy
10 P.T. Barnum, for one
11 When it's noon in Toronto, it's 6:00 PM in ___
12 Arab leader
13 Adele's "Rolling in the ___"
18 Crude dude
22 Sea salt?
25 Drive ___ bargain
26 Benefactor
27 When it's noon in Moscow, it's 9:00 AM in ___
28 *Guys and Dolls* author Runyon
29 Resource
30 Independently
31 Caspar, for one
34 Suffix for Social
40 Intensely sincere
41 Like Louis C.K.
42 "All ___ go!"
43 *Have Gun – Will Travel* hero
45 Det. Taylor of *CSI: NY*
47 Croissant
50 P&L preparers
51 Pitch in
52 Like tropical gardens
53 Posthaste!
54 ___ contendere
55 Common jazz combo
56 In the distance
59 ___ Poke caramel bar

★★★ Word Sudoku

Complete the grid so that each row, each column and each 3 x 3 frame contains the nine letters from the black box below. The hidden nine-letter word is in the diagonal from top left to bottom right.

C E F G I L N T U

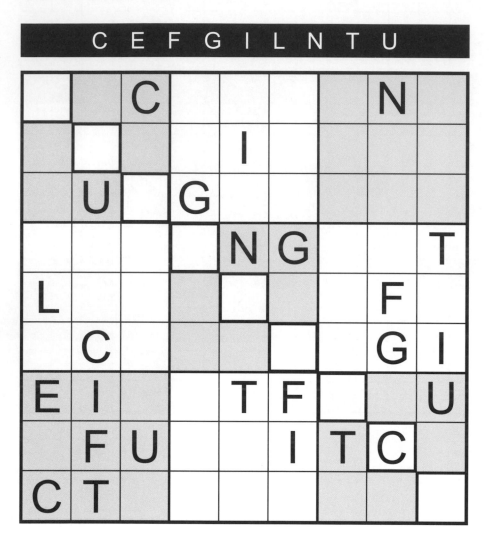

UNCANNY TURN

Rearrange the letters of the phrase below to form a cognate anagram, one which is related or connected in meaning to the original phrase. The answer can be one or more words.

FATAL GRIM MISERY

★ Cage the Animals

Draw lines to completely divide up the grid into small squares with exactly one animal per square. The squares should not overlap.

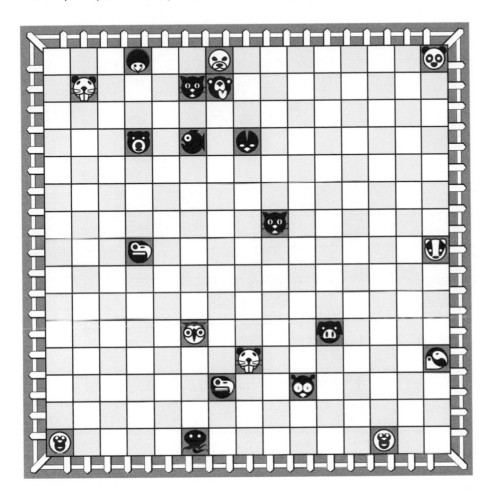

WORD WALL

Beginning at the left side of the wall, make a word by adding one group of letters from each column as you move left to right. When you have found the first word, go back to the second column and start the next word, gathering one group of letters from each column, and so on until all the letters are used to make six words.

★★★★★ World Clock II by John M. Samson

ACROSS

1 Charted records
5 Pool shot
10 Erstwhile ruler
14 Bacchanalian cry
15 Maui greeting
16 King in the *Volsunga Saga*
17 When it's noon in Montreal, it's 9:00 AM in ___
19 Make murky
20 Devout petitions
21 Silk-screen tool
23 Power of the movies
24 Phantom of the Opera
25 Court barriers
27 Where to find woods
30 Non-profit situation
33 *Cosmos* author
35 "Thanks for the Memory" singer
36 Jerry Quarry's 1970 opponent
37 Suffix for court or front
38 Michele of *Glee*
39 Cold medicine
41 The opposition
43 Form of 2,150
44 Dairy case item
46 Exclusive
48 "You ___ seen nothin' yet!"
49 Spoons out
53 Litter mates
56 Boldly courageous
57 At the vertex
58 When it's noon in Rio, it's 8:00 AM in ___
60 Champagne pop?
61 Being of service
62 Five toonies for ___
63 Take-off artist
64 Rescued
65 Orpheus played one

DOWN

1 Spartan field hand
2 Scrimshaw material
3 Start of a Lulu song title
4 Vivaldi subjects
5 Lodestones
6 Tavern tipples
7 Sun
8 "___ a Woman": Beatles
9 NYC's time zone
10 Besmirch
11 When it's noon in Dublin, it's 1:00 PM in ___
12 Et ___ (and others)
13 Small stream
18 Nary a soul
22 Handel's ___ e Leandro

26 Marianne Cope, for one
27 When it's noon in Tokyo, it's 4:00 AM in ___
28 Crude cartel
29 Emulate Big Ben
30 Slothful
31 Mishmash
32 When it's noon in Berlin, it's 7:00 PM in ___
34 Acquire
40 Sprightly
41 *Vanity Fair* humorist Ward
42 Comforted
43 Insurance type
45 Lead-in for form
47 *Le Roi d'Ys* composer
50 Nonclergy

51 Door sign
52 "Just in Time" composer
53 Hemingway's nickname
54 Campus on the Rio Grande
55 Woolly-bear hair
56 Despicable
59 1980 Super Bowl

★★ BrainSnack®—3 by 3s

Which cube set (1–6) should replace the question mark?

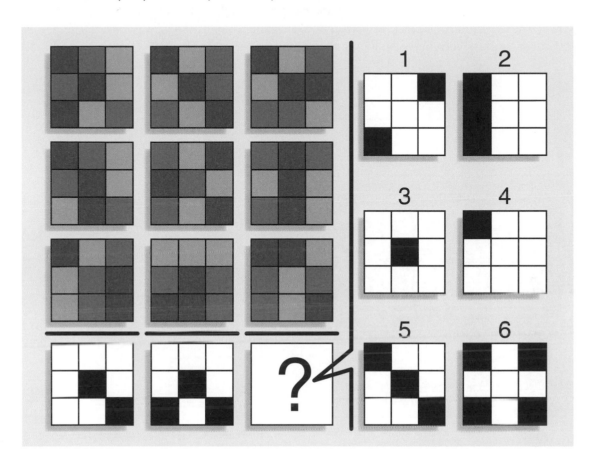

FRIENDS?

What do the following words have in common?

TITLE PAR DIVIDE PLOT MARINE HUMAN

★ Safe Code

To open the safe you have to replace the question mark with the correct figure. You can find this figure by determining the logical method behind the numbers shown. These methods can include calculation, inversion, repetition, chronological succession, or forming ascending and descending series.

SAFE A08

DOODLE PUZZLE

A doodle puzzle is a combination of images, letters and/or numbers that represent a word or a concept. If you cannot solve a doodle puzzle, do not look at the answer right away. Think hard—and outside the box.

★★★★★ New Words of 2012 by John M. Samson

ACROSS

1 ARM adjustment
5 Grinder tooth
10 The avenging Mrs. Peel
14 Sinuous swimmers
15 Glacial spur
16 Out of town
17 Mental lapse*
19 Judge
20 Like a dogfight missile
21 Barbershop foam
23 Shilly-shallies
24 2012 First Family member
25 Weather org.
26 Pedicab kin
29 Fritters away time
32 Box seats
33 One Day ___ Time
34 1970 Australian Open winner
35 Prince William ___
36 Electrical units now called siemens
37 Red Storm Rising org.
38 Revolves
39 The Golden Girls setting
40 Partridge, e.g.
42 Pitch Lake deposit
43 Humpty Dumptyish
44 Big name in cakes
48 iPhone feature
50 "Dream a Little Dream of Me" singer
51 Farm team
52 Final agenda*
54 Guinness measure
55 Harry Truman's birthplace
56 "Waiting for the Robert ___"
57 Concordes
58 Liberty Island neighbor
59 Clearheaded

DOWN

1 Singer McEntire and namesakes
2 Unworldly
3 Warning signal
4 Line from Marathon Man
5 Colorful birds
6 Golden braid
7 Globe Theatre king
8 Chase machine
9 Put back
10 Rare ___ (oxide group)
11 Evil laugh*
12 Endgame ending
13 Yesterday, in Cuba
18 Linguist Chomsky et al.
22 Puts in a request
24 Gemini and Leo
26 Roly-poly
27 Very small matter
28 "What ___ thinking?"
29 Clubber in Rocky III
30 Tasmanian peak
31 Flash of understanding*
32 Peter in Casablanca
35 Appropriate
36 Wonderworks
38 Ski slope transport
39 Charlotte Corday's victim
41 Happenings
42 They crack the whip
44 Port south of Osaka
45 Female boxer Ali
46 German steel city
47 Floral Lauder perfume
48 NYPD Blue roles
49 Line on a graph
50 1950, in copyrights
53 "Friendly Skies" airline: Abbr.

★ Word Pyramid

Each word in the pyramid has the letters of the word above it, plus a new letter.

S

(1) exists
(2) man
(3) danger
(4) worn by women
(5) tricycles
(6) hits
(7) star

DOUBLETALK

Homophones are words that share the same pronunciation, no matter how they are spelled. If they are spelled differently then they are called heterographs. Find heterographs meaning:

UNITS OF LIQUID MEASURE and A MINERAL

★ Hourglass

Starting in the middle, each word in the top half has the letters of the word below it, plus a new letter, and each word in the bottom half has the letters of the word above it, plus a new letter.

(1) navigating
(2) indicate
(3) adjust
(4) part of the digits

(5) long mark
(6) foreign
(7) highland
(8) candy

THREE-IN-ONE

Using all of the letters listed below only once, can you find the names of three Italian cities?

a a a a d e e g l m n o o p p r u

★ Monkey Business

Some of the older students have been monkeying about with the BEST KIDS BOOKS titles list in the library. Can you fix it?

1   A USEFUL TRIBUTE RACE
     by Kami Garcia & Margaret Stohl
2   CHEEKILY MUTTERS
     by Sheila Turnage
3   SHUTEYE AFOOT
     by Ruta Sepetys
4   HAD MELON
     by Cory Doctorow
5   FRANK KOALA IGLOOS
     by John Green

TRIANAGRAM

Three-word groups of anagrams are called triplets or trianagrams.
Complete the group:

S L E E T I N G   _ _ _ _ _ _ _ _   _ _ _ _ _ _ _ _

PAGE 15
Opposite Numbers

F	U	J	I		A	S	L	O	W		O	M	I	T
I	T	E	N		D	I	A	N	A		R	U	D	I
B	A	D	H	A	I	R	D	A	Y		I	S	L	E
S	H	I	E	L	D	E	D		F	E	S	T	E	R
		R	I	A	S		J	A	C	O	B			
P	A	N	I	C	S		P	A	R	T	N	E	R	S
A	B	A	T	E		V	I	D	E	O		N	A	T
L	O	U	S		C	A	P	E	R		M	I	M	I
M	U	G		P	O	S	E	D		M	A	C	O	N
A	T	H	L	E	T	E	S		W	E	R	E	N	T
		T	E	N	T	S		M	A	R	C			
A	L	Y	S	S	A		R	E	F	L	E	C	T	S
S	O	D	S		G	O	O	D	F	E	L	L	A	S
A	L	O	E		E	M	A	I	L		L	I	M	N
P	A	G	E		S	I	N	C	E		O	O	P	S

PAGE 16
BrainSnack®—Keep Turning

Wheel 4. The symbol turns in the opposite direction.

CLOCKWISE

1) PENANCE 2) ABSOLVE
3) RAGTIME 4) SCALENE
5) IDOLIZE 6) MACABRE
7) OCTUPLE 8) NOMINEE
9) IRKSOME 10) ONETIME
11) UKULELE 12) SISTINE
(PARSIMONIOUS)

PAGE 17
Art Trends

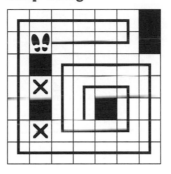

Caravaggisti were stylistic followers of the Italian Baroque painter Caravaggio.

TRIANAGRAM
INGRATE, GRANITE

PAGE 18
Hot and Cold

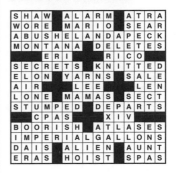

L	A	S	S		B	E	C	O	M	E		A	B	C
O	L	L	A		E	R	O	T	I	C		L	A	H
P	L	A	Y	I	N	G	W	I	T	H	F	I	R	E
S	A	V	I	N	G	S		S	T	O	O	G	E	S
		N	R	A			E	R	N	S	T			
F	R	A	G	I	L	E		S	A	D	E			
L	I	D			L	E	A	K		S	P	A	T	
I	D	I	G		S	I	M	B	A		T	O	D	O
P	E	A	R		H	O	U	R		P	A	N		
		A	B	E	T		A	C	A	D	E	M	Y	
B	I	O	T	A			O	T	E					
E	N	D	I	N	G	S		K	N	O	T	T	E	D
I	C	E	S	T	A	T	I	O	N	Z	E	B	R	A
G	U	T		A	L	U	M	N	I		S	A	I	L
E	S	S		M	A	N	A	G	E		T	R	E	E

PAGE 19
Keep Going

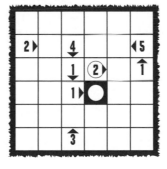

FRIENDS?
Each can have the suffix -ID to form a new word.

PAGE 20
Sport Maze

ONE LETTER LESS OR MORE
GLACIER

PAGE 21
For Good Measure

S	H	A	W		A	L	A	R	M		A	T	R	A
W	O	R	E		M	A	R	I	O		S	E	A	R
A	B	U	S	H	E	L	A	N	D	A	P	E	C	K
M	O	N	T	A	N	A		D	E	L	E	T	E	S
			E	R	I			R	I	C	O			
S	E	C	R	E	T	S		K	N	I	T	T	E	D
E	L	O	N		Y	A	R	N	S		S	A	L	E
A	I	R				L	E	E				L	E	N
L	O	N	E		M	A	M	A	S		S	E	C	T
S	T	U	M	P	E	D		D	E	P	A	R	T	S
		C	P	A	S			X	I	V				
B	O	O	R	I	S	H		A	T	L	A	S	E	S
I	M	P	E	R	I	A	L	G	A	L	L	O	N	S
D	A	I	S		A	L	I	E	N		A	U	N	T
E	R	A	S		H	O	I	S	T		S	P	A	S

PAGE 22
BrainSnack®—Buzzzzz

Bee 3 and 5. The couples have each other's opposite colored stripes on their body.

LETTER LINE
SOOTHSAYER; OYSTER, ASSERT, RASH, EARTHY, TORSO

PAGE 23
Word Sudoku

S	T	E	U	W	P	O	H	R
H	U	O	R	E	T	S	W	P
R	W	P	O	H	S	U	E	T
P	R	H	E	S	O	W	T	U
U	S	T	P	R	W	H	O	E
E	O	W	T	U	H	R	P	S
T	P	R	W	O	U	E	S	H
O	H	U	S	T	E	P	R	W
W	E	S	H	P	R	T	U	O

UNCANNY TURN
CHRISTMAS

PAGE 24
Patriotic Songs

W	A	R	D		D	E	M	O	S		B	O	W	L
A	L	U	I		E	D	I	C	T		O	G	R	E
G	O	D	S	A	V	E	T	H	E	Q	U	E	E	N
S	T	I	L	L	E	R		O	P	U	L	E	N	T
			I	A	L		H	I	D					
J	A	C	K	S	O	N		D	E	T	E	C	T	S
A	L	A	E		P	E	C	A	N		R	A	I	L
U	L	U				P	A	W			C	M	I	
N	A	S	T		C	A	L	E	B		A	T	O	N
T	H	E	R	M	A	L		S	E	N	D	I	N	G
		E	E	N			C	O	M					
A	N	I	M	A	T	E		M	O	D	I	C	U	M
G	O	D	B	L	E	S	S	A	M	E	R	I	C	A
E	V	I	L		E	M	O	T	E		A	T	L	I
S	A	D	E		N	E	S	T	S		L	E	A	N

PAGE 25
Sudoku

6	1	7	2	4	5	3	8	9
3	8	9	6	1	7	4	2	5
4	2	5	8	9	3	7	6	1
2	5	1	7	3	9	6	4	8
7	3	8	4	5	6	9	1	2
9	4	6	1	2	8	5	7	3
8	9	4	3	7	1	2	5	6
5	6	2	9	8	4	1	3	7
1	7	3	5	6	2	8	9	4

SYMBOL SUMS

32 + 8 ÷ 5 x 3 = 24

PAGE 26
Find the Right Word

	F				A	
		C		→		E
L			←			
		I			F	
↗	↗			↓		↑
↗	↑			T		

FACELIFT

CHANGELINGS

C H A L K B O A R D
A S S E S S M E N T
C L A S S R O O M S

PAGE 27
Broadway Musicals I

A	B	A	R		E	T	H	E	L		W	R	A	P
N	A	P	E		M	O	O	L	A		A	A	R	E
T	H	E	B	O	O	K	O	F	M	O	R	M	O	N
S	T	R	U	T	T	E	D		B	U	M	P	E	D
			T	H	E	N		P	A	S	T			
S	L	A	T	E	D		A	E	S	T	H	E	T	E
T	I	M	E	R		K	N	O	T	S		M	A	N
O	V	I	D		L	E	O	N	E		W	E	P	T
M	E	G		D	I	L	L	Y		S	H	E	E	R
P	R	O	B	A	B	L	E		S	H	E	R	R	Y
			I	N	R	I		S	T	A	N			
P	L	I	S	S	E		F	L	O	R	E	N	C	E
S	U	N	S	E	T	B	O	U	L	E	V	A	R	D
I	L	S	E		T	E	N	S	E		E	N	I	D
S	L	O	T		O	A	T	H	S		R	O	S	Y

PAGE 28
Futoshiki

2	3	4	5	1
			V	
5	1 < 3 < 4	2
3	5	1	2	4
			∧	
1	4	2	3	5
				V
4	2	5	1 < 3

LETTERBLOCKS

FOREMAN
PLUMBER

PAGE 29
BrainSnack®—Veg Choice

Vegetable 5. The vegetable at the bottom is not in the set above.

QUICK CROSSWORD

		B		J	I	G		S			
S	A	L	S	A		I		O		L	A
P		U		Z		G	R	O	U	P	I	E		L
I		E		Z		I		L		A	L	T
N		S		S		G			P	A	D		O

PAGE 30
Pizza

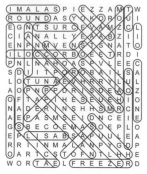

Pizza was originally invented in Naples, Italy, and the dish has since become popular in many parts of the world.

DELETE ONE

Delete F and find LOTTERY WIN

PAGE 31
Broadway Musicals II

M	O	L	E		D	A	N	C	E		B	A	S	E
E	D	E	N		O	N	I	O	N		A	L	A	N
S	I	N	G	I	N	I	N	T	H	E	R	A	I	N
H	E	S	I	T	A	T	E		A	N	G	E	L	A
			N	A	L	A		A	N	T	E			
S	H	I	E	L	D		A	N	C	E	S	T	O	R
T	O	B	E	Y		T	U	N	E	R		H	U	E
O	N	E	R		R	I	G	I	D		M	O	T	E
I	D	A		R	E	N	E	E		S	O	L	E	D
C	O	M	P	O	S	E	R		P	O	L	E	R	S
			A	M	O	S		A	I	D	E			
S	A	M	U	E	L		A	L	L	O	C	A	T	E
T	H	E	S	O	U	N	D	O	F	M	U	S	I	C
E	S	M	E		T	H	A	N	E		L	I	N	T
M	O	O	D		E	L	M	E	R		E	N	Y	O

PAGE 32
Spot the Differences

DOUBLETALK

HALL/HAUL

PAGE 33
Sudoku X

7	1	3	9	5	6	4	2	8
8	2	4	7	1	3	6	5	9
6	5	9	8	2	4	1	3	7
4	3	5	6	7	2	8	9	1
1	6	8	5	4	9	2	7	3
2	9	7	3	8	1	5	4	6
5	8	6	4	9	7	3	1	2
3	7	1	2	6	5	9	8	4
9	4	2	1	3	8	7	6	5

BLOCK ANAGRAM
MASTERMIND

PAGE 34
Similar Starts

C	O	W	L		D	A	U	N	T		A	H	E	M
O	H	I	O		E	L	V	E	S		P	U	C	E
H	A	L	L	O	F	F	A	M	E		P	L	O	D
E	R	M	I	N	E	S		O	T	H	E	L	L	O
N	E	A	T	E	N			S	E	T	H			
		A	I	D	E		S	E	R	I	O	U	S	
S	S	H		L	E	G	A	L		S	T	U	N	T
A	T	I	P		R	A	B	A	T		E	S	T	A
N	O	L	A	N		D	O	N	U	T		E	O	N
G	A	L	L	O	N	S		T	R	E	S			
		C	O	L	A		T	R	I	V	I	A		
M	E	L	M	O	T	H		B	U	R	N	I	N	G
A	L	I	I		H	E	L	L	R	A	I	S	E	R
L	I	M	N		A	M	O	U	R		S	I	R	E
L	U	B	U		N	I	T	R	O		E	T	T	E

PAGE 35
BrainSnack®—Letter Pairs

TU. From top to bottom each block has consecutive letters.

QUICK WORD SEARCH

N	E	E	R	C	S	E	D	I	W	E	L	B	A	C
R	E	L	I	R	H	T	S	A	R	T	N	O	C
E	M	I	T	B	R	O	A	D	C	A	S	T	B	X
J	N	Y	E	U	G	O	L	A	N	A	M	A	R	D
E	T	I	B	D	N	U	O	S	G	N	I	T	A	R

PAGE 36
Kakuro

9	8	7	■	1	6	2
8	6	3	■	2	4	1
7	■	2	9	4	3	5
■	5	1	8	■	1	■
4	8	■	2	3	■	■
1	3	■	1	8	4	2
9	6	8	■	9	8	5

DOUBLETALK
CEILING/SEALING

PAGE 37
Similar Endings

F	A	R	R		V	O	T	E	D		E	M	M	A
A	L	O	E		E	C	O	L	E		C	O	O	S
B	E	A	C	O	N	H	I	L	L		S	T	O	W
E	R	M	I	N	E	S		A	U	S	T	E	R	E
R	O	S	T	E	R			D	E	A	L			
			E	R	A	S		S	E	E	T	H	E	D
A	L	B		S	T	A	R	T		S	I	E	V	E
P	O	O	H		E	L	I	A	S		C	L	O	D
E	M	B	E	D		S	P	R	A	Y		L	E	E
S	A	B	R	I	N	A		R	U	E	D			
		Y	O	R	E			T	A	I	C	H	I	
A	C	H	I	E	V	E		N	E	S	T	L	E	S
N	O	U	N		A	L	B	E	R	T	H	A	L	L
T	I	L	E		D	A	M	O	N		E	H	I	E
A	L	L	S		A	L	I	N	E		R	E	O	S

PAGE 38
Sudoku Twin

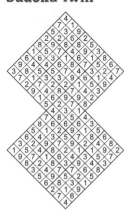

TRIANAGRAM
MADDEN, DAMNED

PAGE 39
Hourglass

(1) stalker, (2) skater, (3) stake, (4) take, (5) cake, (6) creak, (7) racket, (8) tracker

SANDWICH
WORK

PAGE 40
Primate Puzzle

B	A	R	D		P	L	A	T	H		T	S	A	R
O	M	O	O		L	O	R	R	E		H	U	M	E
O	M	A	N		A	D	A	I	R		E	L	A	N
M	O	N	K	E	Y	I	N	G	A	R	O	U	N	D
			E	L	I			L	E	M				
B	U	O	Y	A	N	T		A	D	V	E	R	B	S
I	M	A	S		G	R	O	S	S		N	E	A	T
P	B	S				E	D	H			C	R	Y	
O	R	E	S		O	N	S	E	T		R	O	I	L
D	A	S	T	A	R	D		S	I	L	E	N	C	E
		A	N	A				G	Y	M				
P	L	A	N	E	T	O	F	T	H	E	A	P	E	S
H	O	L	D		I	N	E	R	T		I	T	T	O
E	R	T	E		O	L	L	I	E		N	A	N	A
W	E	A	R		N	Y	L	O	N		G	H	A	R

PAGE 41
Sport Maze

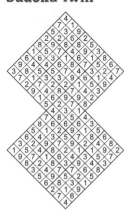

ONE LETTER LESS OR MORE
UNDRESS

PAGE 42
BrainSnack®—Shape Shifter

Group 4. In all the other groups the isolated dot is located in the lower left.

DOODLE PUZZLE
BigShot

PAGE 43
2012 Ryder Cup

S	M	E	E		P	A	T	C	H		O	M	A	N
E	A	R	L		A	T	R	I	A		Y	A	L	E
T	I	G	E	R	W	O	O	D	S		S	T	O	A
S	L	O	V	E	N	L	Y		T	I	T	T	E	R
			A	B	E	L		D	E	R	E	K		
S	I	L	T	E	D		B	A	N	K	R	U	P	T
C	R	U	E	L		T	O	T	E	S		C	O	E
O	A	K	S		R	O	W	E	D		T	H	I	S
U	T	E		M	E	N	E	S		B	O	A	S	T
R	E	D	E	E	M	E	R		C	A	R	R	E	Y
		O	A	T	E	R		C	A	N	T			
T	I	N	G	E	D		S	A	N	T	I	A	G	O
I	C	A	L		I	A	N	P	O	U	L	T	E	R
R	A	L	E		E	N	U	R	E		L	E	N	T
E	N	D	S		D	E	G	A	S		A	N	T	S

PAGE 44
Walt Disney

Walt Disney created Donald Duck seven years after creating Mickey Mouse.

FRIENDS?
Each can have the prefix HIGH- to form a new word.

PAGE 45
Word Sudoku

L	Y	X	G	A	B	R	I	T
R	I	G	L	Y	T	X	B	A
T	B	A	X	R	I	Y	G	L
G	R	T	B	X	Y	A	L	I
A	L	Y	T	I	R	G	X	B
I	X	B	A	G	L	T	Y	R
B	T	R	Y	L	X	I	A	G
Y	G	I	R	B	A	L	T	X
X	A	L	I	T	G	B	R	Y

UNCANNY TURN
A TUB OF ICE CREAM

PAGE 46
Binairo

I	O	I	O	I	O	I	I	O	I	O	O
O	I	O	O	I	I	O	O	I	O	I	I
O	O	I	I	O	O	I	I	O	O	I	I
I	I	O	O	I	O	I	O	I	I	O	O
O	O	I	I	O	I	O	O	I	I	O	I
O	I	O	O	I	I	O	I	O	O	I	I
I	O	I	I	O	O	I	I	O	O	I	O
O	O	I	O	O	I	I	O	I	I	O	I
I	I	O	I	I	O	O	I	O	O	I	O
I	I	O	I	O	I	O	O	I	O	I	I
O	O	I	O	O	I	I	O	I	O	I	I
I	I	O	I	I	O	O	I	O	I	O	O

CHANGELINGS
ANTAGONIST
BESTSELLER
CHARACTERS

PAGE 47
Independence

B	O	A	R		T	R	A	D	E		S	C	A	D
A	C	R	E		H	I	R	E	D		T	U	N	A
S	T	A	T	U	E	O	F	L	I	B	E	R	T	Y
H	A	B	I	T	S		S	O	C	R	A	T	E	S
			R	I	T	A		S	T	O	L			
F	O	R	E	C	A	S	T		S	K	I	R	T	S
E	P	I		A	N	T	I	C		E	N	U	R	E
T	E	S	H		D	I	N	A	H		G	L	O	W
C	R	E	E	D		R	E	M	A	P		E	V	E
H	A	R	L	E	M		D	E	M	A	N	D	E	D
			P	L	O	Y		O	M	N	I			
A	T	H	L	E	T	E	S		E	I	G	H	T	S
F	R	E	E	D	O	M	M	A	R	C	H	E	R	S
A	I	R	S		R	E	E	V	E		T	R	O	N
R	O	S	S		S	N	E	A	D		S	E	T	S

PAGE 48
Horoscope

WORD WALL
CHARACTERISTICALLY, IRREVERSIBILITY, ELECTROCUTED, MENDICANT, TORRID, TAN

PAGE 49
BrainSnack®—Twinkle Twinkle

Star 8. All the other stars are reflected in the water.

SYMBOL SUMS
$12 \div 3 \times 4 - 12 = 4$

PAGE 50
Longings

C	O	V	E		S	A	M	B	A	S		A	B	A
A	D	I	T		Q	U	E	A	S	Y		R	U	N
W	I	S	H	F	U	L	T	H	I	N	K	I	N	G
S	N	A	I	L	E	D		T	A	O	I	S	T	S
			C	I	A			D	O	E	S	T		
W	H	I	S	T	L	E		C	A	S	S			
H	A	T			D	R	A	M		K	N	O	B	
A	L	E	C		L	I	O	N	S		S	A	V	E
M	E	M	O		O	T	T	O		N	E	T		
			P	T	A	H		N	E	P	T	U	N	E
S	W	A	T	H			N	A	H					
P	A	L	E	R	M	O		B	T	W	E	L	V	E
A	S	T	R	E	E	T	C	A	R	N	A	M	E	D
I	T	E		E	N	T	I	R	E		S	N	A	G
N	E	R		D	E	S	I	R	E		P	O	L	E

PAGE 51
Sudoku

9	5	4	7	1	6	2	3	8
8	7	2	3	9	4	1	6	5
3	6	1	8	2	5	7	9	4
2	1	5	9	8	3	4	7	6
4	8	6	5	7	1	3	2	9
7	9	3	4	6	2	8	5	1
6	4	7	2	5	8	9	1	3
1	3	9	6	4	7	5	8	2
5	2	8	1	3	9	6	4	7

TRIANAGRAM
PINES, SPINE

PAGE 52
Number Cluster

7	7	7	7	5	3
7	7	5	5	5	3
8	7	5	6	4	3
8	2	8	6	4	4
8	2	8	6	6	4
8	8	8	1	6	6

CHANGELINGS

P A I N T B R U S H
E X H I B I T I O N
L A N D S C A P E S

PAGE 53
From the Heart

W	E	R	E		D	U	M	P	S		P	L	A	T
E	L	A	L		E	L	I	O	T		R	O	N	A
L	O	V	E	I	S	A	L	L	A	R	O	U	N	D
S	P	E	C	T	E	R		E	N	E	M	I	E	S
H	E	L	T	E	R				L	O	I	S		
			R	A	T	S		M	E	S	S	I	A	H
L	O	L	A		S	T	R	A	Y		E	A	V	E
A	D	E			A	Y	N			N	O	B		
P	I	E	R		Y	I	E	L	D		P	A	N	E
D	E	M	E	T	E	R		Y	O	N	O			
			A	G	H	A			L	E	N	O	R	E
C	A	N	N	E	R	E		L	U	A	I	H	E	D
L	O	V	E	A	N	D	M	A	R	R	I	A	G	E
O	N	I	T		E	D	U	C	E		A	R	A	N
D	E	N	S		D	A	M	E	S		C	A	N	S

PAGE 54
Concentration—Lateral Thinking

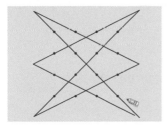

LETTER LINE

ASSOCIATION; OASIS, COINS, CASINO, ACTION, COAST

PAGE 55
BrainSnack®—Color Palette

Paint 3. Paint 1 was used twice to color in 50% of a surface. Paint 2 was used once to color in 50% and once to color in less than 50%. Therefore paint 3 was used once to color in 50% of a surface and once to color in more than 50% of a surface.

CLOCKWISE

1) STRATUM
2) UNIFORM
3) BLOSSOM
4) TOPONYM
5) EARWORM
6) REALISM
7) ROSTRUM
8) ABRAHAM
9) NAUSEAM
10) EPIGRAM
11) ANTONYM
12) NOSTRUM (SUBTERRANEAN)

PAGE 56
Angelina Jolie

A	N	I	T	A		P	I	K	E	R		E	L	A	L
R	U	H	R		A	N	I	T	A		N	O	M	E
A	L	E	A		P	U	S	H	I	N	G	T	I	N
B	U	T	C	H	E	R	S		L	E	A	S	E	D
			O	H	A	R	E		B	R	A	G		
S	P	U	N	K	Y		P	R	O	T	E	C	T	S
E	E	R	I	E		F	L	E	A	S		H	O	W
A	R	I	D		F	R	E	E	D		S	A	R	I
T	D	S		C	L	E	A	N		P	A	N	T	S
O	U	T	D	O	O	R	S		B	A	R	G	E	S
			W	A	R	E		S	L	I	D	E		
S	E	D	A	T	E		A	M	A	R	I	L	L	O
P	L	A	Y	I	N	G	G	O	D		N	I	A	S
C	O	R	N		C	O	O	K	E		I	N	L	A
A	N	N	E		E	R	N	E	S		A	G	A	R

PAGE 57
Printing

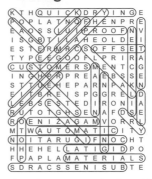

The platen press is the oldest type of printing press; the paper is pressed onto the form with the help of a plate.

DELETE ONE

Delete E and find A FANTASY FILM

PAGE 58
Futoshiki

| 4 | 3 | 1 | 5 | 2 |
| 1 < 2 < 3 < 4 < 5 |
2	4	5	1	3
3	5 > 4	2 > 1
5	1	2	3 < 4

SYMBOL SUMS

7 − 2 ÷ 1 × 4 = 20

PAGE 59
Alec Baldwin

A	N	N	A		R	I	P	U	P		S	T	Y	E
F	O	A	M		A	N	I	S	E		C	H	O	W
T	H	E	A	V	I	A	T	O	R		H	E	R	E
			R	O	N	N	Y		F	O	L	D	E	R
O	R	B	I	T	E	D		T	E	P	E	E		
F	E	E	L	E	R		R	E	C	A	P	P	E	D
F	I	E	L	D		B	E	R	T	H		A	T	E
I	N	T	O		S	E	E	R	S		P	R	E	P
N	E	L		I	T	A	L	Y		M	E	T	R	O
G	R	E	M	L	I	N	S		R	O	D	E	N	T
			J	E	L	L	O		B	E	T	I	D	E	S
C	O	U	R	S	E		R	E	B	E	C			
A	B	I	G		T	H	E	G	E	T	A	W	A	Y
L	I	C	E		T	O	T	A	L		B	O	L	A
L	E	E	R		O	W	E	N	S		S	O	A	K

Keep Going

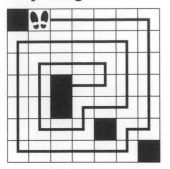

TRIANAGRAM
STRAP, TRAPS

Sport Maze

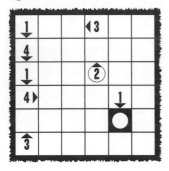

ONE LETTER LESS OR MORE
GRANITE

Coast to Coast

B	U	R	R		R	A	M	P	S		W	E	N	T
A	T	E	E		E	P	C	O	T		E	R	O	O
B	E	A	C	H	V	O	L	L	E	Y	B	A	L	L
A	P	P	L	I	E	D		A	P	O	S	T	L	E
		U	N	A			P	U	T					
T	R	E	S	T	L	E		C	E	R	E	A	L	S
H	O	S	E		S	A	P	I	D		R	E	E	K
U	S	S			R	A	G			R	O	I		
M	I	E	N		A	T	R	A	S		D	I	N	E
B	E	N	E	A	T	H		R	E	P	R	E	S	S
		U	R	L			C	O	O					
P	O	N	T	I	A	C		S	U	P	P	O	S	E
S	H	O	R	E	S	O	F	T	R	I	P	O	L	I
I	R	M	A		E	A	R	L	E		E	L	A	N
S	E	E	L		S	T	O	O	D		D	A	V	E

BrainSnack®—Castle Conundrum

Angle 4. The chain of the drawbridge is too long.

BLOCK ANAGRAM
ROCK PAPER SCISSORS

Word Sudoku

M	O	I	N	R	A	T	Y	H
H	A	N	T	O	Y	I	R	M
R	Y	T	M	H	I	A	O	N
Y	T	H	R	A	N	M	I	O
O	M	A	Y	I	H	N	T	R
I	N	R	O	T	M	Y	H	A
N	I	M	H	Y	R	O	A	T
T	H	Y	A	M	O	R	N	I
A	R	O	I	N	T	H	M	Y

UNCANNY TURN
PROMOTION

Binairo

I	O	I	I	O	O	I	O	I	I	O
O	I	O	I	O	I	O	I	O	I	I
O	O	I	O	I	I	O	I	I	O	I
I	I	O	O	I	O	I	O	I	I	O
I	O	I	I	O	I	O	I	O	O	I
O	O	I	I	O	I	I	O	I	O	I
I	I	O	O	I	O	I	I	O	I	O
O	I	O	I	I	O	O	I	I	O	I
I	O	I	O	O	I	I	O	O	I	I
O	I	I	O	I	I	O	I	I	O	O
I	I	O	I	I	O	I	O	O	I	O

SANDWICH
BOARD

Facial Features

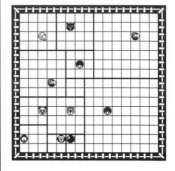

Cage the Animals

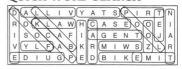

WORD WALL
CONCEPTUALIZATIONS, DEMOCRATIZATION, OBSTETRICIAN, CURTAILED, RENOWN, BED

BrainSnack®—Familiar Faces

Figure 5 is shown 3 times as a three-in-a-row.

QUICK WORD SEARCH

PAGE 69

XXXs

S	L	I	D		D	E	C	A	Y		I	B	E	T
P	A	G	E		I	T	A	L	O		N	A	V	E
C	H	O	C	O	L	A	T	E	K	I	S	S	E	S
A	R	R	I	V	A	L		C	O	N	T	E	N	T
		D	A	T		O	D	E	S	S	A			
L	E	V	E	L	E	D		E	N	Y	A			
E	L	I	S		D	I	S	C	O		D	E	R	N
A	M	C			A	I	L				L	Y	E	
N	O	E	L		U	N	C	A	P		S	L	A	W
		O	S	S	A		T	A	R	T	A	N	S	
A	S	T	U	T	E			N	O	R				
S	T	E	R	I	L	E		O	C	T	O	P	U	S
H	U	N	D	R	E	D	S	M	A	C	K	E	R	S
E	P	E	E		S	N	E	A	K		E	R	S	T
N	E	T	S		S	A	C	R	E		S	E	A	S

PAGE 70

Ball Sports

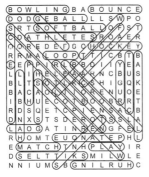

Ball sports are described in Chinese texts dating from the third millennium BC.

DELETE ONE

Delete O and find A VALENTINE CARD

PAGE 71

Word Wheel

bad, ban, bat, bid, bin, bio, bit, boa, nab, tab, bait, band, bind, boat, bond, tomb, baton, bandit, obtain, badminton.

LETTERBLOCKS

MUSCLES
STOMACH

PAGE 72

A Common Bond

A	R	I	D		S	T	A	M	P		O	D	O	R
D	E	S	I		H	A	N	O	I		P	A	P	A
I	A	N	F	L	E	M	I	N	G		E	V	E	N
A	R	T	F	U	L		S	T	E	E	R	I	N	G
		E	C	T	O		H	O	N	E	D			
A	N	G	R	I	E	S	T		N	O	T	B	A	D
B	O	A		D	R	A	W	L		S	T	O	G	Y
E	R	R	S		S	K	I	E	S		A	W	O	L
L	A	Y	T	O		A	N	T	A	L		I	R	A
S	H	O	R	T	S		E	U	R	O	P	E	A	N
		L	A	I	K	A		P	A	G	E			
P	E	D	I	C	U	R	E		S	A	B	L	E	S
H	Y	M	N		L	O	N	D	O	N	B	O	R	N
I	R	A	E		K	L	E	P	T		L	A	M	A
L	E	N	D		S	E	R	T	A		E	M	A	G

PAGE 73

Do the Math

4	×	6	÷	8	=	3
−		+		−		
3	+	2	−	5	=	0
×		÷		+		
7	×	1	+	9	=	16
=		=		=		
7		8		12		

DOUBLETALK

CHEWS/CHOOSE

PAGE 74

BrainSnack®—Team Game

Team C. The order of the weakest to the strongest team is: D A E B C. The final match is played between C and B.

DOODLE PUZZLE

eLBow

PAGE 75

2012 Movies

A	M	O	S		S	M	A	S	H		S	K	A	T
B	A	T	H		C	U	L	P	A		T	E	R	I
C	L	O	U	D	A	T	L	A	S		O	V	A	L
D	I	S	T	O	R	T		S	T	E	R	I	L	E
		O	I	L			I	M	I	N				
D	E	B	U	T	E	D		B	L	U	E	J	A	Y
I	C	E	T		T	R	U	L	Y		S	A	T	O
V	O	N			I	L	I				M	A	G	
E	L	A	T		P	L	U	M	P		D	E	L	I
R	E	F	U	S	A	L		P	R	A	I	S	E	S
		F	R	E	T			E	R	G				
C	E	L	T	I	C	S		A	V	A	R	I	C	E
O	R	E	L		H	A	L	L	E	B	E	R	R	Y
L	I	C	E		E	L	L	E	N		S	M	E	E
A	S	K	S		S	A	D	A	T		S	A	W	S

PAGE 76

Safe Code

15   78   63
↓ −4   ↓ −4   ↓ −4
11   74   59

CHANGELINGS

S U P E R N O V A S
A S T R O N O M E R
T E L E S C O P E S

PAGE 77

Word Pyramid

(1) MD, (2) mad, (3) damn,
(4) amend, (5) daemon,
(6) abdomen, (7) Doberman

DOUBLETALK

REIN/REIGN

PAGE 78

Sudoku

6	9	5	1	2	4	7	8	3
1	3	7	9	8	6	4	5	2
2	8	4	5	7	3	9	6	1
3	7	6	8	4	2	1	9	5
8	1	2	3	9	5	6	7	4
5	4	9	6	1	7	3	2	8
9	6	8	2	3	1	5	4	7
4	5	1	7	6	8	2	3	9
7	2	3	4	5	9	8	1	6

SYMBOL SUMS

$13 + 10 − 5 ÷ 9 = 2$

PAGE 79
How Sad

```
C A L F | G R A T A | A B B A
A L A R | R U R A L | U L A R
B L U E P E N C I L | S U I T
S A D D L E S | L I S T E N S
      D A T |   S E R B
C A B I N E T | N O X I O U S
O G L E | D O Y E N | A N T E
L O U | M E W | N I A
O R E L | T A T E R | C E L L
R A P I E R S | R E B A T E S
      R O T O | T A L
O M I N O U S | M U R I E L S
V I N E | B L U E R I B B O N
A N T S | L E N I N | E R T E
L A S S | E D E N S | R O S E
```

PAGE 80
Futoshiki

```
2   5   1   3 < 4
            v     ^
3   1   4   2   5

5 > 4 > 2 > 1   3

1   3   5   4   2
    v   v       v
4   2   3   5   1
```

CHANGELINGS
G A S T R O N O M Y
S O M M E L I E R S
C O R D O N   B L E U

PAGE 81
BrainSnack®—On Ice

M–L–Q–P–O–K–N–J–G. The leafstalk and the top of the leaf on the puck alternately point in the direction of the next puck.

WORD WALL
ENTREPRENEURIALISM,
HEARTBREAKINGLY,
TESTOSTERONE, TRADEMARK,
CEDARS, TON

PAGE 82
James Bond Villains

```
T E D S | V O I D S | E S M E
A S I A | I N L E T | S C A D
R A O U L S I L V A | K A Y E
P U R S U I T | A N D I R O N
      A L T |   L O M A
H A G G L E D | B E C O M E S
A L O E | D E C O Y | S A D E
S O L | F U R | N I N
T O D D | S O D O M | S G T S
A F F A B L E | N A S T A S E
      I S E E |   T E A
M O N T A N A | M A R T I A N
O L G A | D R J U L I U S N O
L E E R | E L E N I | E N D S
L O R D | R O D I N | S T Y E
```

PAGE 83
Picnic

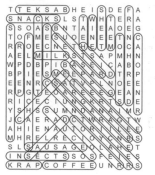

The ideal season to go on a picnic is summer, when there is lots of sun.

DELETE ONE
Delete E and find LEADING MAN

PAGE 84
Sport Maze

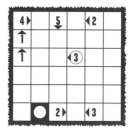

ONE LETTER LESS OR MORE
ROUNDED

PAGE 85
Red

```
E L L E | S P R A T | E W E R
L O A F | C A I R O | N I N E
S W I F T A L B U M | G L I B
E S C O R T S | M A T I L D A
      R E T |   T O N I
C O S T N E R | M O D E S T Y
H S T | T R I P E | D E F O E
A S O R | S A R A H | R I M A
R I P E N | N O R A S | L E R
D E S C E N T | A R T E M I S
      I O N A |   M I R
R E G R E S S | A L F R E D O
B E N D | S H A M E F A C E D
I R A E | E U R U S | N C A A
S O L D | R E A R S | D E N Y
```

PAGE 86
Letter Soup

Stomach, Brain, Artery, Finger, Kidney, Diaphragm, Tongue, Muscle

THREE-IN-ONE
ERIE, VICTORIA, BAIKAL

PAGE 87
Sudoku X

```
6 7 1 8 4 3 2 9 5
8 2 5 6 9 7 3 4 1
4 3 9 5 2 1 6 8 7
7 5 6 4 1 9 8 2 3
9 4 2 3 7 8 5 1 6
1 8 3 2 6 5 9 7 4
2 6 8 7 3 4 1 5 9
5 1 4 9 8 6 7 3 2
3 9 7 1 5 2 4 6 8
```

BLOCK ANAGRAM
MONOPOLY

PAGE 88
1950s Song Hits

```
D E C O | S A P I D | R B I S
E S A U | E N U R E | E Y R E
E A R T H A N G E L | T E A L
P I L L O W S | D E C I B E L
      I N E |   T O N Y
B L A N K E T | R E Q U E S T
R I L E | D I V A S | E L I A
I L L | T A T | O R U
N A S T | L A T E R | E V E N
E C H E L O N | S E G M E N T
      O L A N |   P R E
B I O L O G Y | E T E R N A L
R A K E | H O T D I G G I T Y
A M U R | O N E I L | E T O N
T A P S | T O R T E | D A N N
```

PAGE 89

BrainSnack®—Pop Numbers

4. The sum of the stamps of the same color always equals 10. 1 + 9, 10 + 0, 3 + 7, 6 + 4.

QUICK CROSSWORD

PAGE 90

Do the Math

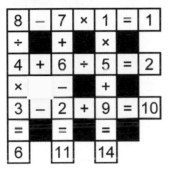

TRIANAGRAM

CUTER, CRUET

PAGE 91

1960s Song Hits

O	S	L	O		L	A	P	S	E		S	M	E	W
S	T	A	R		E	R	I	C	A		L	O	R	E
S	U	G	A	R	S	U	G	A	R		A	O	N	E
A	B	S	T	A	I	N		B	L	E	N	D	E	D
		O	V	O			I	N	D	Y				
S	A	B	R	I	N	A		D	E	S	E	R	V	E
A	L	L			M	E	A	R		R	I	E	L	
U	L	U		A	D	Z			V	I	A			
D	E	E	F		S	H	E	R		G	E	N	T	
I	N	V	E	N	T	S		D	I	V	E	R	S	E
	E	L	A	L			O	O	N					
C	O	L	E	M	A	N		O	R	L	E	A	N	S
A	L	V	A		S	O	L	D	I	E	R	B	O	Y
R	E	E	S		E	L	I	O	T		A	R	O	N
L	A	T	E		S	A	B	R	A		L	I	N	E

PAGE 92

Kakuro

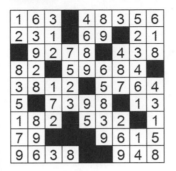

DOUBLETALK

REEK/WREAK

PAGE 93

Sudoku Twin

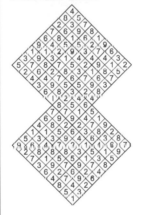

TRIANAGRAM

ROPED, DOPER

PAGE 94

BrainSnack®—A Bad Year?

1967. All the other years are formed with the same figures.

CLOCKWISE

1) HUNGARY 2) ODYSSEY
3) RAGGEDY 4) TRADEGY
5) IMAGERY 6) COMPANY
7) URUGUAY 8) LOYALTY
9) TERSELY 10) UNCANNY
11) RICKETY 12) ECONOMY
(HORTICULTURE)

PAGE 95

1970s Song Hits

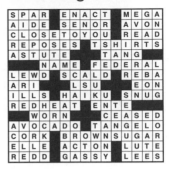

PAGE 96

Poetry

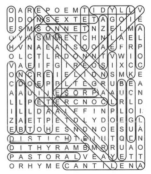

A poem does not have to follow a fixed meter and definitely does not have to rhyme.

DELETE ONE

Delete N and find PRIVATE JET

PAGE 97

Hourglass

(1) Beatles, (2) stable, (3) bleat, (4) able, (5) ball, (6) label, (7) liable, (8) liberal

UNCANNY TURN

DOCILE AS A MAN TAMED IT

PAGE 98
1980s Song Hits

M	A	S	K		C	L	E	A	N		E	R	G	O
E	R	I	E		L	I	L	L	I		D	O	O	M
N	I	N	E	T	O	F	I	V	E		A	C	T	A
D	E	S	P	I	S	E		A	L	A	S	K	A	N
			E	M	E				S	I	N	O		
I	M	P	R	E	S	S		B	E	N	E	F	I	T
D	A	H	S		T	I	M	O	N		R	A	R	E
O	S	O				R	O	Y				G	E	N
L	O	T	S		C	E	D	E	D		S	E	N	T
S	N	O	O	P	E	D		R	E	P	O	S	E	S
			G	A	I	N			C	U	M			
H	A	R	N	E	S	S		L	I	C	E	N	S	E
E	G	A	D		U	P	S	I	D	E	D	O	W	N
R	I	P	S		R	E	E	S	E		A	M	A	D
S	O	H	O		E	D	I	T	S		Y	E	N	S

PAGE 99
Maze—Alternate Colors

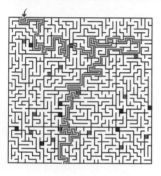

FRIENDS?
They are all words attributed to Charles Dickens.

PAGE 100
Word Parts

OBJECTIVE, ABDOMINAL, TELESCOPE, PAPERCLIP, MAGNETRON, EDUCATION

ONE LETTER LESS OR MORE
NOSTALGIC

PAGE 101
Familiarity

W	A	R	S		P	A	S	H	A		E	M	I	T
E	R	I	C		E	R	R	E	D		D	A	T	A
B	O	B	R	E	D	F	O	R	D		U	T	E	P
B	E	S	I	D	E	S		E	L	E	C	T	R	A
			B	I	S				E	L	A	M		
O	B	J	E	C	T	S		E	D	I	T	O	R	S
A	L	I		T	A	L	O	N		S	E	D	A	N
T	A	M	S		L	I	N	D	A		D	I	M	E
E	M	M	E	T		T	E	E	M	S		N	P	R
R	E	A	P	E	R	S		R	E	Q	U	E	S	T
			D	A	T	E			T	U	N			
F	A	I	R	E	S	T		S	H	A	R	P	E	N
E	L	S	A		T	O	M	M	Y	W	O	L	F	E
L	O	O	T		E	R	I	E	S		L	E	T	S
L	U	N	E		R	O	G	E	T		L	A	S	T

PAGE 102
BrainSnack®—Red Blooded

Blood cell 2. The middle circle is missing in the core with the small circle.

LETTER LINE
GUIDELINES; LEGEND, SLEDGE, DEIGN, NUDGE, GUILE

PAGE 103
Word Sudoku

C	E	R	N	K	T	L	V	O
V	O	L	E	R	C	K	T	N
T	K	N	O	L	V	C	R	E
R	T	K	V	C	N	E	O	L
O	N	V	K	E	L	R	C	T
L	C	E	T	O	R	N	K	V
E	V	O	R	N	K	T	L	C
N	R	C	L	T	O	V	E	K
K	L	T	C	V	E	O	N	R

THREE-IN-ONE
IRVING, HAWTHORNE, WHARTON

PAGE 104
This and That

C	U	P	S		B	A	L	S	A		P	E	E	L
O	P	A	H		I	L	I	A	D		U	G	L	I
S	P	R	I	N	G	T	I	M	E		P	Y	L	E
T	E	E	N	A	G	E		S	L	I	P	P	E	D
A	R	R	I	V	E				I	C	E	T		
			N	E	S	S		A	N	Y	T	I	M	E
S	M	O	G		T	E	R	S	E		S	A	R	A
T	O	P				A	S	H				N	I	S
O	O	P	S		E	L	T	O	N		P	S	S	T
P	R	O	C	E	S	S		T	U	L	L			
		R	O	T	C				C	E	A	S	E	S
R	E	T	R	E	A	D		A	L	A	S	K	A	N
E	T	U	I		P	E	R	C	E	N	T	A	G	E
M	A	N	N		E	L	I	H	U		I	L	E	A
O	L	E	G		S	I	D	E	S		C	A	R	D

PAGE 105
Sudoku

1	5	4	7	8	9	6	3	2
3	7	6	2	4	1	5	9	8
9	8	2	3	5	6	1	7	4
2	4	5	1	6	3	7	8	9
8	1	7	9	2	5	4	6	3
6	3	9	4	7	8	2	5	1
5	2	3	6	9	4	8	1	7
7	9	8	5	1	2	3	4	6
4	6	1	8	3	7	9	2	5

SYMBOL SUMS
$52 - 4 \div 6 \times 5 = 40$

PAGE 106
Word Ladders

help, pole, lose, lens, send, desk

light, legit, agile, glide, oldie, lodge, globe

SANDWICH
PHONE

PAGE 107
Eclectic Mix

C	L	A	D		B	L	E	E	P		W	H	A	M
R	O	L	E		L	E	A	V	E		E	I	R	E
A	R	I	S	T	O	C	R	A	T		S	L	I	T
B	E	N	E	A	T	H		S	E	T	T	L	E	S
S	N	E	R	T			R	A	E	S				
			T	E	N	T		O	S	T	R	I	C	H
F	T	C		R	O	S	E	S		E	N	D	U	E
I	H	O	P		M	A	R	I	O		S	E	T	A
J	O	N	A	H		R	E	E	L	S		S	E	T
I	N	G	R	E	S	S		R	E	N	D			
			E	T	L	A			O	U	T	R	E	
D	U	R	N	I	N	G		S	A	U	T	E	E	D
I	S	E	E		D	A	L	M	A	T	I	A	N	S
V	E	E	R		A	M	O	U	R		E	S	T	E
E	E	L	S		L	E	D	G	E		S	E	A	L

PAGE 108
Futoshiki

3	4	2	5	1
4 < 5	3	1	2
1	3 < 4	2	5
2 > 1	5 > 3 < 4
5	2 > 1	4	3

LETTERBLOCKS

ACROBAT
TRAPEZE

PAGE 109
BrainSnack®—Angles

Piece 3. To be useful, the top purple square of piece 3 must shift left.

DOODLE PUZZLE

TeaCup

PAGE 110
Carnivorans

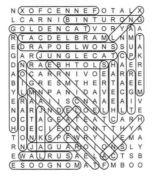

Not all carnivorans are carnivores; the panda is a vegetarian that primarily eats bamboo.

DELETE ONE

Delete N and find ASTROLOGY CHART

PAGE 111
Paradise

G	A	R	B		G	A	P	E	D		T	E	A	L
A	S	E	A		A	M	O	R	E		S	A	N	E
S	H	A	N	G	R	I	L	A	S		E	S	T	E
P	E	R	S	O	N	S		S	P	U	T	T	E	R
			H	U	E			I	N	S	O			
A	L	B	E	R	T	O		E	S	T	E	F	A	N
R	I	L	E	D		V	I	D	E	O		E	V	E
O	N	U	S		R	A	P	I	D		A	D	E	E
S	E	E		S	E	T	O	N		S	N	E	R	D
E	N	H	A	N	C	E		A	C	C	E	N	T	S
			E	L	I	A			L	A	C			
P	R	A	T	T	L	E		W	O	N	D	E	R	S
H	A	V	E		L	A	K	E	U	T	O	P	I	A
I	C	E	R		E	V	E	N	T		T	E	A	M
L	E	N	S		D	E	N	T	S		E	E	L	S

PAGE 112
Spot the Differences

DOUBLETALK

DONE/DUN

PAGE 113
Word Wheel

any, aye, eye, lay, yea, yen, only, yang, yoga, agony, leggy, gangly, genealogy.

DOODLE PUZZLE

PAintBall

PAGE 114
Themeless

M	A	M	A		R	I	Y	A	L		S	M	E	E
A	L	I	I		A	R	E	N	A		T	A	R	N
H	A	N	K	Y	P	A	N	K	Y		E	S	T	O
A	N	I	M	A	T	E		A	E	R	A	T	E	S
N	A	S	A	L			R	I	D	E				
			N	I	N	O		A	S	P	I	R	E	R
A	Y	R		E	T	H	Y	L		E	L	S	I	E
B	O	Y	S		H	A	M	E	L		Y	O	R	E
A	G	A	T	E		R	A	R	E	E		N	E	D
S	I	N	A	T	R	A		T	A	T	S			
			O	N	T	O			H	I	R	E	S	
B	A	N	D	A	N	A		A	N	A	T	O	L	E
A	R	E	A		A	B	E	L	I	N	C	O	L	N
N	E	A	R		L	I	L	A	C		O	N	E	S
G	O	L	D		D	E	A	N	E		M	E	R	E

PAGE 115
BrainSnack®—Snow Fun

Snow flake 6. The star in its center has six points; the others have five.

WORD WALL

CONTRADISTINCTIONS, CORRESPONDENCES, PORTRAITISTS, TABLEWARE, LETHAL, KEY

PAGE 116
The Puzzled Librarian

1. *Wise Men*
2. *The Dinner*
3. *After Visiting Friends*
4. *Coolidge*
5. *Insane City*
6. *The Burn Palace*
7. *Detroit*
8. *Ghostman*
9. *The Light Between Oceans*
10. *Rules of Civility*

DOODLE PUZZLE

MegaByte

PAGE 117
Themeless

PAGE 120
Olio

PAGE 123
Color Blind

PAGE 118
Hourglass

(1) exclaim, (2) malice, (3) camel,
(4) calm, (5) camp, (6) cramp,
(7) camper, (8) compare

SYMBOL SUMS

$38 \div 2 + 18 - 4 = 33$

PAGE 121
Sport Maze

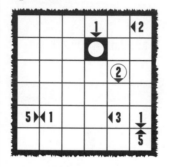

CHANGELINGS

L I T E R A T U R E
P H I L O S O P H Y
J O U R N A L I S M

PAGE 124
Zoo

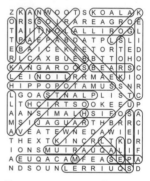

Zoos are a great place to relax but their main goal is to keep animals threatened with extinction safe and sound.

DELETE ONE

Delete P and find CINDERELLA STORY

PAGE 119
Maze—Binoculars

FRIENDS?

Each can have the suffix -RON to form a new word.

PAGE 122
BrainSnack®—No Graffiti

Spray can 2. According to the table of comparison, the following symbols have the following values: black square = 8, white circle and white square = 4, black star and black circle = 2 and white star = 1.

BLOCK ANAGRAM

STRATEGO

PAGE 125
Word Sudoku

G	D	I	R	N	O	U	E	A
E	A	U	G	D	I	R	O	N
O	N	R	E	U	A	G	I	D
I	U	N	D	R	G	E	A	O
A	O	D	I	E	U	N	G	R
R	E	G	A	O	N	D	U	I
N	G	O	U	A	D	I	R	E
D	I	E	O	G	R	A	N	U
U	R	A	N	I	E	O	D	G

UNCANNY TURN
THE DAILY HATE

PAGE 126
Futoshiki

3	4	5	2	1
4	5	1	3	2
2	3	4	1	5
5	1	2	4	3
1	2 < 3	5 > 4

TRIANAGRAM

LAMBING, AMBLING

PAGE 127
Hidden Forest

```
S P A R   A T E A M   R O M O
P U C E   B A N T U   E V E R
C L O A K R O O M S   F E T A
A P P L I E S   S T I R R E D
      I T A   A N E W
S O F T E S T   C R A S H E S
U G L Y   T R E A D   H E L P
A D A   I A L   L S U
V E S T   O I I E R   E M I R
E N H A N C E   B E R N S F N
    D I E T   C E E
A B A N D O N   A L A M O D E
T E N T   P O R C U P I N E S
L A C E   U N I T S   E E L S
I R E D   S E N S E   S A L E
```

PAGE 128
Horoscope

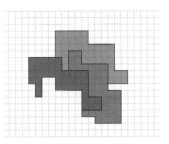

WORD WALL

ELECTROCARDIOGRAPH,
PHARMACOLOGISTS,
SINGLEHANDED, GERMINATE,
MAIDEN, USE

PAGE 129
BrainSnack®—Time Gap

1:30 p.m.

LETTERBLOCKS

DIVORCE
VERDICT

PAGE 130
Historic Homes

```
B O A R   A R A R A T   L A P
A A R E   S A T I R E   O R A
T H O M A S J E F F E R S O N
T U N I S I A   E S T E E M S
      S T S   E S S A Y
D E N S I T Y   M A R C
E L A   E L A M   U S E R
A L M A   E N E M Y   E L M O
D E E D   S T A B   O I D
    M A T A   A R C H E R S
S T A I D   E A U
T I G R E S S   A S I N I N E
E R N E S T H E M I N G W A Y
E E E   T I E R E D   R A V E
P S S   E R M I N E   Y S E R
```

PAGE 131
Sudoku

7	1	3	9	6	2	5	8	4
5	9	2	8	1	4	6	3	7
4	8	6	7	5	3	1	9	2
3	4	5	1	2	7	9	6	8
9	6	1	4	3	8	7	2	5
8	2	7	5	9	6	4	1	3
1	5	8	3	4	9	2	7	6
6	7	9	2	8	5	3	4	1
2	3	4	6	7	1	8	5	9

SYMBOL SUMS

$64 - 8 \div 8 + 11 = 18$

PAGE 132
Number Cluster

7	7	7	7	7	7
7	6	5	5	2	2
6	6	6	5	8	4
6	1	6	5	8	4
3	3	3	5	8	4
8	8	8	8	8	4

SANDWICH

HAND

PAGE 133
Sitcom Pilots

```
M A C E   C A R L A   V E T O
A R A N   A D E E R   I V O R
Y A R D   P A N I C   S I N K
A L L I N T H E F A M I L Y
    N Y U   D E B
B A D G E R S   B E L L O W S
A M U S   E A R L S   E C H O
S A Y   B O A   H E R
I T E M   P R I M A   S E E R
S I N A T R A   E L D E R L Y
    H O I   B E L
  T W O A N D A H A L F M E N
J O I N   C A N O N   I O T A
O R L E   E L E N I   S T O P
T I D Y   S I T K A   H O N E
```

PAGE 134
Concentration—Gridlock

DOODLE PUZZLE

MisUnderStandInG

PAGE 135

BrainSnack®—On the Green

E5. Both vertically and horizontally there is a golf ball in the middle between two flags.

CLOCKWISE

1) NARWHAL 2) ODDBALL
3) MICHAEL 4) ESPAÑOL
5) NUPTIAL 6) CYNICAL
7) LIBERAL 8) AUSTRAL
9) TEARFUL 10) UNCIVIL
11) RAPHAEL 12) EYEBALL
(NOMENCLATURE)

PAGE 136

TV Quotes

M	A	T	E		C	A	R	A	T		C	O	B	B
A	S	E	T		A	D	A	I	R		A	G	U	E
T	H	E	H	O	N	E	Y	M	O	O	N	E	R	S
S	E	M	I	N	O	L	E		P	A	C	E	R	S
		O	S	E	E		M	I	T	A				
G	R	A	P	E	S		R	E	C	E	N	T	L	Y
L	E	G	I	T		S	A	T	A	N		R	E	O
A	G	R	A		C	A	V	I	L		D	O	O	D
R	A	E		S	A	L	E	S		B	O	O	N	E
E	L	E	M	E	N	T	S		C	O	M	P	E	L
		A	W	A	Y		S	A	R	I				
S	T	A	G	E	D		B	L	U	E	N	O	S	E
T	H	E	P	R	I	C	E	I	S	R	I	G	H	T
L	A	R	I		A	P	A	C	E		O	R	I	N
O	T	O	E		N	A	M	E	D		N	E	V	A

PAGE 137

Sleep

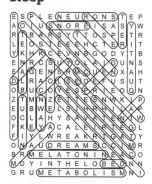

Sleep is a way to protect the body because exhaustion will physically wreak your body in the long run.

FRIENDS?

Each can have the suffix -SOME to form a new word.

PAGE 138

Sudoku X

9	4	7	5	6	2	3	8	1
3	8	6	9	4	1	2	5	7
1	5	2	7	3	8	4	9	6
2	6	4	3	8	9	7	1	5
8	1	5	6	7	4	9	2	3
7	9	3	2	1	5	6	4	8
5	7	8	4	2	6	1	3	9
4	3	9	1	5	7	8	6	2
6	2	1	8	9	3	5	7	4

BLOCK ANAGRAM

SOLITAIRE

PAGE 139

The Simpsons

L	A	H	R		C	H	E	E	R		E	D	A	M
A	L	I	E		L	E	V	E	E		S	E	M	I
R	U	T	H	P	O	W	E	R	S		K	W	A	N
D	I	S	E	A	S	E	S		P	R	I	E	S	T
		A	G	E	D		R	O	O	M	Y			
S	A	B	R	E	S		G	O	N	D	O	L	A	S
A	M	A	S	S		S	O	U	S	E		A	N	I
K	O	B	E		A	L	A	T	E		C	R	E	E
E	L	Y		A	B	A	T	E		H	O	G	A	N
S	E	G	M	E	N	T	S		S	E	N	O	R	A
		E	U	R	O	S		R	E	F	S			
M	I	R	R	O	R		P	O	I	T	I	E	R	S
O	M	A	R		M	O	E	S	Z	Y	S	L	A	K
M	I	L	A		A	N	N	I	E		T	A	V	I
A	N	D	Y		L	A	D	E	D		S	L	E	D

PAGE 140

Maze—Beehive

SANDWICH

HORSE

PAGE 141

Sport Maze

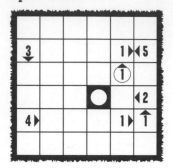

ONE LETTER LESS OR MORE

YOUNGSTER

PAGE 142

BrainSnack®—Slippery

5. The skin's color pattern consists of black alternated with a colored square. There is always a red square between two identically colored squares.

LETTER LINE

OPALESCENT; NESTLE, STAPLE, APOSTLE, SPLEEN, ANTELOPE, EASEL

PAGE 143

B as in ...

B	A	R	N		M	A	N	O	R		A	B	R	A
A	L	O	U		U	L	N	A	E		B	A	I	L
B	A	Y	M	A	S	T	E	R	S		A	D	D	A
E	S	S	E	N	C	E		S	T	A	N	D	E	E
		R	A	L			I	N	D	Y				
D	E	B	A	T	E	D		E	N	D	O	W	E	D
E	L	U	L		S	E	L	I	G		N	A	R	A
U	L	M			A	I	D			G	U	T		
C	A	P	P		P	L	I	E	D		N	O	P	E
E	S	K	I	M	O	S		R	E	P	E	N	T	S
		I	G	E	T			F	E	E				
G	E	N	E	R	A	L		S	E	N	D	I	N	G
A	L	P	O		B	A	C	K	A	N	I	M	A	L
E	L	I	N		L	I	M	I	T		N	I	N	O
L	E	E	S		E	R	I	N	S		G	N	A	W

PAGE 144
Word Sudoku

A	C	L	G	H	S	T	E	I
I	T	S	E	A	L	H	G	C
G	E	H	T	C	I	L	S	A
E	A	C	L	G	H	S	I	T
T	S	I	A	E	C	G	H	L
H	L	G	S	I	T	C	A	E
S	G	E	C	T	A	I	L	H
L	I	T	H	S	E	A	C	G
C	H	A	I	L	G	E	T	S

THREE-IN-ONE

CHICAGO, LES MISÉRABLES, WICKED

PAGE 145
Kakuro

DOUBLETALK

FLEW/FLUE

PAGE 146
Bank Holiday

B	A	R	T		S	T	A	I	N		A	N	T	S
A	D	A	H		C	H	U	T	E		F	O	A	M
S	A	F	E	H	O	U	S	E	S		F	A	C	E
E	M	E	R	A	L	D		A	T	T	A	C	H	E
		A	I	D			L	A	I	C				
R	E	H	I	R	E	D		B	E	D	R	O	O	M
A	M	E	N		D	O	M	E	S		S	U	R	E
S	D	A		L	A	H				N	O	G		
T	E	D	S		A	T	E	A	M		E	T	N	A
A	N	T	H	E	M	S		N	I	L	S	S	O	N
	E	U	R	O			R	E	T					
S	O	L	D	I	E	R		P	A	C	H	I	S	I
H	O	L	D		B	O	D	Y	C	H	E	C	K	S
A	L	E	E		A	T	O	L	L		R	E	A	M
G	A	R	R		E	S	T	E	E		S	S	T	S

PAGE 147
Sudoku Twin

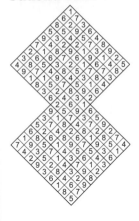

TRIANAGRAM

PRESTO, POSTER

PAGE 148
BrainSnack®—Pot Luck

N. Each vowel is followed by the letter that precedes it in the alphabet.

QUICK CROSSWORD

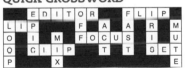

PAGE 149
Pick a Number

M	I	S	S		W	R	A	P	S		E	F	T	S
I	O	T	A		A	I	S	L	E		D	O	R	E
T	W	E	N	T	Y	F	O	U	R		W	R	E	N
T	A	N	G	E	N	T		S	E	D	A	T	E	D
		U	N	E			N	A	R	Y				
B	U	S	I	E	S	T		H	A	R	D	E	S	T
A	R	E	N	T		A	B	I	D	E		I	P	O
S	A	V	E		A	L	O	N	E		E	G	O	S
I	N	E		A	D	O	B	E		M	A	H	D	I
C	O	N	D	E	M	N		S	H	O	R	T	E	R
	T	E	R	I			A	N	N					
B	O	Y	C	O	T	T		A	T	T	I	R	E	D
A	R	T	E		T	H	I	R	T	Y	N	I	N	E
S	E	W	N		E	E	R	I	E		G	A	T	E
S	L	O	T		D	E	T	E	R		S	L	E	D

PAGE 150
Swimming

Swimming is seen as a very healthy form of recreation because it uses almost every muscle.

DOUBLETALK

BALL/BAWL

PAGE 151
Do the Math

9	−	3	+	7	=	13
−		+		−		
6	+	4	−	1	=	9
+		−		+		
5	−	2	+	8	=	11
=		=		=		
8		5		14		

LETTERBLOCKS

KETCHUP
PRETZEL

PAGE 152
Placement Test

B	A	U	M		M	E	T	R	O		D	A	T	E
A	B	R	A		A	V	A	I	L		E	N	I	D
B	E	G	I	N	N	I	N	G	O	F	T	I	M	E
S	T	E	N	C	I	L		G	R	E	A	T	E	N
			L	O	A				L	I	A	R	S	
T	A	B	A	S	C	O		A	N	I	L			
A	R	O	N		N	I	N	O	N		C	H	A	
M	I	D	D	L	E	O	F	T	H	E	R	O	A	D
S	A	Y		A	R	N	I	E			E	L	I	A
			O	S	E	E		S	I	L	V	E	R	Y
A	D	A	P	T			N	E	E					
H	A	R	P	O	O	N		A	C	T	R	E	S	S
E	N	D	O	F	D	I	S	C	U	S	S	I	O	N
A	D	E	S		O	C	H	E	R		A	N	T	I
D	Y	N	E		R	E	E	D	S		L	E	S	T

PAGE 153
Futoshiki

5	2	3	1	4
1	4	5	2	3
2 < 3 < 4 < 5	1
4	1	2 < 3	5
3 < 5	1	4 > 2

CHANGELINGS

L I G H T H O U S E
S K Y S C R A P E R
C L O C K T O W E R

PAGE 154
BrainSnack®—Odd Block

Group 5. In each group, the value on the letter, number or color block indicates the numerical difference between each other. For example, in group 1, there is a different of 1 between 1 and 2 AND B and C. In group 2, red equals red AND 4 equals 4. In group 5, the letters are three places and the numbers are two places away from each other.

QUICK WORD SEARCH

T	R	A	I	L	Z	M	R	H	L	A	K	E	L	K
R	I	F	H	C	A	E	B	O	O	K	C	V	E	A
U	U	S	A	P	L	A	N	E	O	T	D	A	T	E
N	F	M	I	A	T	S	A	O	C	M	E	E	O	R
K	P	C	X	V	P	H	O	T	O	U	R	L	M	B

PAGE 155
Playing the Market

A	M	O	I		C	H	I	L	D		C	R	E	W
M	A	N	N		A	U	R	A	E		H	E	L	I
P	R	E	F	E	R	R	E	D	S	T	O	C	K	S
S	K	I	L	L	E	T		D	E	S	I	R	E	E
			A	L	F			R	A	C	E			
A	M	A	T	E	U	R		S	T	R	E	A	K	S
R	A	S	E		L	A	G	O	S		S	T	U	N
A	N	T			D	A	L			I	D	I		
B	I	R	D		M	A	L	T	A		R	O	O	D
S	C	O	O	T	E	R		I	N	C	E	N	S	E
		N	O	R	M			T	A	P				
S	T	O	R	I	E	S		W	I	L	L	I	A	M
C	O	M	M	O	N	K	N	O	W	L	E	D	G	E
A	R	E	A		T	I	A	R	A		T	E	A	M
T	E	R	N		O	T	T	E	R		E	E	R	O

PAGE 156
Find the Right Word

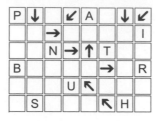

PAINTBRUSH

CHANGELINGS

T O O T H B R U S H
B U B B L E B A T H
A F T E R S H A V E

PAGE 157
Word Ladders

hard, raid, liar, sail, silk, disk

ocean, dance, cedar, cider, drive, diner, liner

TRIANAGRAM

REPAINT, PERTAIN

PAGE 158
Sudoku

7	6	4	2	5	3	9	1	8
1	3	5	8	4	9	7	2	6
2	8	9	1	6	7	4	5	3
4	1	8	3	2	5	6	9	7
3	7	6	9	1	8	2	4	5
9	5	2	4	7	6	3	8	1
8	2	1	6	3	4	5	7	9
5	4	3	7	9	1	8	6	2
6	9	7	5	8	2	1	3	4

SYMBOL SUMS

$1 \times 23 - 7 \div 4 = 4$

PAGE 159
C-

B	U	L	B		A	M	A	Z	E		T	R	I	G
O	S	E	E		G	A	M	I	N		E	A	R	N
L	E	A	N	L	I	V	I	N	G		E	S	A	U
D	E	F	E	A	T	S		C	L	O	T	H	E	S
			F	H	A				A	L	E	C		
T	S	H	I	R	T	S		A	N	D	R	O	I	D
E	L	A	T		E	L	A	N	D		S	U	R	E
S	E	I			I	R	T			R	O	N	
T	E	R	M		O	P	T	I	C		S	S	N	S
A	P	P	E	A	R	S		C	H	I	N	E	S	E
		E	N	I	D				I	N	A			
P	A	R	T	N	E	R		S	E	C	R	E	T	S
O	R	S	O		R	E	S	T	F	A	L	L	E	N
N	O	O	R		E	N	R	O	L		E	S	A	I
D	O	N	S		D	O	I	L	Y		D	A	R	T

PAGE 160
Maze—Traffic Grid

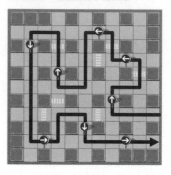

FRIENDS?

Each can have the prefix TRANS-to form a new word.

PAGE 161
BrainSnack®—Stack 'em

2B. Stack B belongs in location 2. Per stack the colors shift two places down.

DOODLE PUZZLE

SumMer

PAGE 162

F-

M	A	R	C		F	U	M	E	S		T	H	A	T
O	P	A	H		O	R	A	L	E		Y	O	D	A
S	I	T	A		L	I	P	F	L	O	P	P	E	D
H	E	B	R	I	D	E	S		A	L	I	E	N	S
			R	A	V	E	L		S	W	A	N		
E	R	O	D	E	D		S	P	A	N	G	L	E	S
F	E	T	E	S		B	E	A	R	D		E	E	C
R	A	H	S		H	E	A	R	D		H	A	L	O
E	T	E		T	O	R	T	E		L	A	M	E	R
M	A	R	C	E	L	L	O		T	I	R	A	D	E
		O	P	I	E		S	O	L	A	R			
P	R	O	B	E	D		S	P	R	I	N	K	L	E
A	I	R	W	E	A	T	H	E	R		G	E	E	R
L	A	C	E		Y	O	U	R	E		U	T	E	S
S	L	A	B		S	O	L	O	S		E	S	S	E

PAGE 163

Fencing

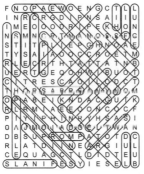

Fencing is a modern sport that requires a combination of physical and strategic qualities.

SANDWICH
BIRD

PAGE 164

Sport Maze

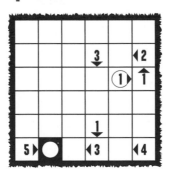

BLOCK ANAGRAM
RED KANGAROO

PAGE 165

World Clock I

C	O	W	S		S	A	M	O	S		S	C	A	D
O	M	I	T		A	L	E	R	T		H	O	M	E
C	A	S	A	B	L	A	N	C	A		O	P	I	E
O	N	E	R	O	U	S		A	N	T	W	E	R	P
			L	O	T			D	A	M	N			
A	D	M	I	R	E	D		A	B	R	A	H	A	M
H	O	O	T		D	A	I	S	Y		N	A	P	A
A	N	N			M	S	S				G	A	G	
R	O	T	E		C	O	M	E	S		P	E	R	U
D	R	E	A	M	O	N		T	Y	R	A	N	T	S
			C	R	A	M			S	O	L			
C	H	A	N	C	E	L		A	T	L	A	N	T	A
P	E	R	E		D	U	S	S	E	L	D	O	R	F
A	L	L	S		I	S	L	A	M		I	L	I	A
S	P	O	T		C	H	O	P	S		N	O	O	R

PAGE 166

Word Sudoku

I	L	C	U	E	T	G	N	F
G	N	F	F	I	L	U	T	C
T	U	F	G	C	N	I	E	L
F	E	I	L	N	G	C	U	T
L	G	T	I	U	C	E	F	N
U	C	N	T	F	E	L	G	I
E	I	G	C	T	F	N	L	U
N	F	U	E	L	I	T	C	G
C	T	L	N	G	U	F	I	E

UNCANNY TURN
GRIMM'S FAIRY TALE

PAGE 167

Cage the Animals

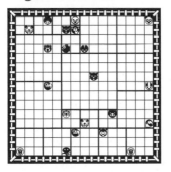

WORD WALL
DISPROPORTIONATELY,
TEMPERAMENTALLY, PLAUSIBILITY,
CATHARTIC, ERRAND, END

PAGE 168

World Clock II

H	I	T	S		M	A	S	S	E		T	S	A	R
E	V	O	E		A	L	O	H	A		A	T	L	I
L	O	S	A	N	G	E	L	E	S		R	O	I	L
O	R	I	S	O	N	S		S	T	E	N	C	I	L
T	Y	R	O	N	E			E	R	I	K			
			N	E	T	S		P	R	O	S	H	O	P
L	O	S	S			S	A	G	A	N		H	O	P	E
A	L	I			I	E	R				L	E	A	
Z	I	N	C		A	N	T	I	S		M	M	C	L
Y	O	G	H	U	R	T		S	O	L	E			
			A	I	N	T			L	A	D	L	E	S
P	U	P	P	I	E	S		V	A	L	I	A	N	T
A	T	O	P		M	E	X	I	C	O	C	I	T	Y
P	E	R	E		U	T	I	L	E		A	T	E	N
A	P	E	R		S	A	V	E	D		L	Y	R	E

PAGE 169

BrainSnack®—3 by 3s

Set 4. Per column, place the three squares on top of each other. If the three small squares on top of each other are orange and blue then you get a black square at the bottom, otherwise it is white.

FRIENDS?

Each can have the prefix SUB- to form a new word.

PAGE 170

Safe Code

352 ← 176

↑ ×2

22 → 44 → 88

DOODLE PUZZLE
WestErn

PAGE 171

New Words of 2012

R	E	F	I		M	O	L	A	R		E	M	M	A
E	E	L	S		A	R	E	T	E		A	W	A	Y
B	R	A	I	N	C	R	A	M	P		R	A	T	E
A	I	R	T	O	A	I	R		L	A	T	H	E	R
S	E	E	S	A	W	S		S	A	S	H	A		
			A	M	S		R	I	C	K	S	H	A	W
L	O	A	F	S		L	O	G	E	S		A	T	A
A	S	H	E		S	O	U	N	D		M	H	O	S
N	S	A		T	U	R	N	S		M	I	A	M	I
G	A	M	E	B	I	R	D		T	A	R			
		O	V	A	T	E		S	A	R	A	L	E	E
C	A	M	E	R	A		M	A	M	A	C	A	S	S
O	X	E	N		B	U	C	K	E	T	L	I	S	T
P	I	N	T		L	A	M	A	R		E	L	E	E
S	S	T	S		E	L	L	I	S		S	A	N	E

PAGE 172
Word Pyramid

(1) is, (2) sir, (3) risk, (4) skirt,
(5) trikes, (6) strikes, (7) asterisk

DOUBLETALK
QUARTS/QUARTZ

PAGE 173
Hourglass

(1) sailing, (2) signal, (3) align,
(4) nail, (5) line, (6) alien,
(7) alpine, (8) praline

THREE-IN-ONE
GENOA, PADUA, PALERMO

PAGE 174
Monkey Business

1. *Beautiful Creatures*
2. *Three Times Lucky*
3. *Out of the Easy*
4. *Homeland*
5. *Looking for Alaska*

TRIANAGRAM
STEELING, GENTILES

ANSWERS TO QUICK AND DO YOU KNOW

p 15 Spain
p 17 Libreville
p 19 *Philadelphia*
p 21 Lisa del Giocondo (Gherardini)
p 23 Esperanto
p 25 Georges Bizet
p 27 Romulus and Remus
p 29 Orion
p 31 Africa
p 33 Rudyard Kipling
p 35 Andrew Lloyd Webber (music) and Tim Rice (lyrics)
p 37 Blue
p 39 John Singer Sargent
p 41 David Lynch
p 43 Six
p 45 Curling
p 47 Elizabeth Taylor
p 49 Fencing
p 51 Havana
p 53 Hawaii (Kealakekua Bay)
p 55 Etta James
p 57 Clarified butter
p 59 *Snow White and the Seven Dwarfs*
p 61 Boston Bruins, Chicago Blackhawks, Detroit Red Wings, Montreal Canadiens, New York Rangers, Toronto Maple Leafs
p 63 Iceland
p 65 Jupiter
p 67 *The Silence of the Lambs*
p 69 South Africa
p 71 Three (One Summer Games [Montreal 1976], two Winter Games [Calgary 1988; Vancouver 2010])
p 73 Castor and Pollux
p 75 In King Arthur's Court
p 77 Philip K. Dick
p 79 Ottawa
p 81 Austrian
p 83 The Library of Alexandria
p 85 Jean Sibelius
p 87 Au
p 89 Cross-country skiing and rifle shooting
p 91 Woody Allen
p 93 Pakistan and China
p 95 Eagle and snake
p 97 Bamboo spear
p 99 Edith Wharton
p 101 Bono
p 103 1989
p 105 Roy Lichtenstein
p 107 *Robinson Crusoe*
p 109 Roosevelt
p 111 Carole King
p 113 Archery
p 115 Agatha Christie
p 117 Gold (in Australia)
p 119 Greece
p 121 Frank Lloyd Wright
p 123 The 1930s
p 125 William Carlos Williams
p 127 Sting
p 129 Ravi Shankar
p 131 Lindy Hop
p 133 Sicily
p 135 Katharine Hepburn
p 137 Sahara
p 139 White
p 141 Sesame
p 143 Alicia Keys
p 145 Malé
p 147 *Twelfth Night*
p 149 Genoa, Italy
p 151 Lincoln
p 153 Roger Maris
p 155 Green
p 157 Alva
p 159 Bette Davis
p 161 Saul Bellow
p 163 A lion
p 165 Sri Jayawardenapura Kotte
p 167 A sun (the Sun of May)
p 169 Ukraine
p 171 Sn
p 173 New York Giants